INTRODU

The
Enlightenment

Lloyd Spencer and Andrzej Krauze

Edited by Richard Appignanesi

TOTEM BOOKS

First published in the United States in 1997 by Totem Books
Inquiries to PO Box 223, Canal Street Station
New York, NY 10013

Distributed to the trade in the United States
by National Book Network Inc.,
4720 Boston Way, Lanham, Maryland 20706

Originating editor: Richard Appignanesi

ISBN 1 874166 56 0

Library of Congress Catalog Card Number: 96-061950

Printed and bound in Great Britain by
Biddles Ltd., Guildford and King's Lynn

Let There Be Light . . .

The Enlightenment was an intellectual current that galvanized Europe during the course of the 18th century. Centred in Paris, it spread itself across the whole of Europe to the American colonies. Networks of writers and thinkers gave the 18th century a remarkable intellectual coherence.

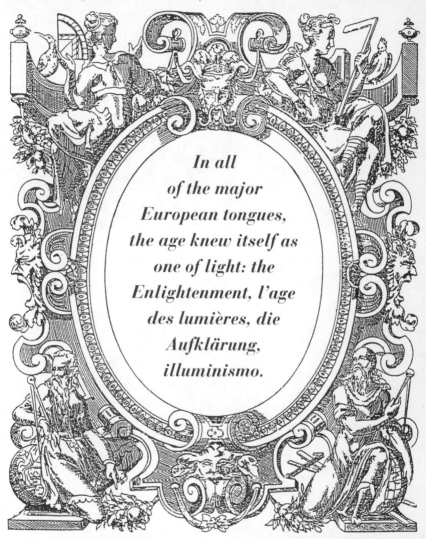

In all of the major European tongues, the age knew itself as one of light: the Enlightenment, l'age des lumières, die Aufklärung, illuminismo.

The intellectuals of the Enlightenment felt themselves to be part of a great movement representing the highest aspirations and possibilities of mankind. They were reformers who believed their cause was best served by the new passion for argument, criticism and debate.

The Radiance of the Absolute Monarchs

In France, the reigns of the Absolutist monarchs, **Louis XIII** (1601–43), **Louis XIV** – the "Sun King" – (1638–1715), **Louis XV** (1710–74) and **Louis XVI** (1754–93) made Paris the cultural capital of the world and, at the same time, created both an audience and a target for the reforming zeal of the French Enlightenment.

The Enlightenment spoke French, literally its *lingua franca*. Anything published in French was immediately accessible to educated society all over Europe. Important works not originally written in French were soon translated into the universal language. Across the world "men of letters" declared themselves to be the disciples of French writers.

Paris, the Capital of the Enlightenment

This was as true for David Hume and Adam Smith from Scotland as it was for Benjamin Franklin and Thomas Jefferson from the American colonies, or Cesare Beccaria from Milan. They knew they had "arrived" when they were accepted in the *salons* of Paris.

In all of continental Europe, court society and the wealthy bourgeoisie looked to France as the model of taste.

FRANCE SETS THE TONE IN LITERATURE, ART AND ARCHITECTURE.

AND ALSO IN MANNERS, COOKING AND DRESS. FRENCH FASHION IS THE EPITOME OF CIVILIZATION!

A Sussex landowner wrote to his son: "A man who understands French may travel all the World over without hesitation of making himself understood, and may make himself perfectly agreeable to all Good Company, which is not the case of any other Language whatever."

Beginnings of the Light

"There is a mighty light which spreads itself over the world, especially in those two free nations of England and Holland, on whom the affairs of all Europe now turn." Lord Shaftesbury's letter to Le Clerc, 6 March 1706

For much of the 17th century, Holland was the most liberal country in Europe. Amsterdam provided a refuge for freethinkers and religious dissidents of all kinds. In 1667, the English philosopher **John Locke** (1632–1704) composed an *Essay on Toleration*. He had been closely associated with Protestant plotters against the rule of the Catholic King **James II** (1633–1701).

There Locke concentrated on his major works, his *Essay Concerning Human Understanding* and *Two Treatises of Government*. Both books were to remain central to the debates that raged throughout the Age of Enlightenment.

England's "Glorious Revolution"

Continued resistance to James II's pro-Catholic activities caused the English parliament to invite the Dutch Protestant, **William III** of Orange (1650–1702) and his English wife **Mary II** (1662–94), to take over the English throne. They sailed from Holland and did so in the bloodless – hence "Glorious" – Revolution of 1688.

This definitively established the sovereignty of the English parliament and gave England a "Bill of Rights". Other reforms soon made England the most free and liberal country in Europe. The Toleration Act (1689) allowed most Protestant Dissenters, including such sects as the Quakers, to worship freely, but not to hold public office. The Church of England lost its monopoly of religious worship and education, and the last vestiges of its control over the press in 1695.

An Age of Revolutions

The two great cosmopolitan capitals, Paris and London, both grew dramatically during the 18th century. But England's commercial muscle meant that London progressed much more. During the first half of the century, England experienced an agricultural revolution. In the latter part of the century, the industrial revolution gained pace.

IN *1776*, THE AGE DREW TO A CONCLUSION WITH A REVOLUTION *AGAINST* ENGLAND BY ITS AMERICAN COLONISTS.

IN *1789*, THE UPHEAVAL OF THE FRENCH REVOLUTION FINALLY CHANGED EVERYTHING.

a Versailles a Versailles du 5 Octobre 1789.

These revolutions attempted to put the principles of the Enlightenment into practice.

Coffee-houses, Social Clubs and Journalism

This was also an age of public sociability and a journalism of ideas. Coffee-houses were the focal point of intellectual life in London. By 1740, there were more than 400 in the area of Westminster alone. The new Bank of England and the East India trading company used coffee-houses. Lloyd's coffee-house in 1691 became Lloyd's of London, the centre of marine insurance.

Locke's "Tabula Rasa"

Throughout the 18th century, the essential book for philosopher and non-philosopher alike was John Locke's *Essay Concerning Human Understanding* (1690). For almost all of the thinkers of the Enlightenment, one philosophical tenet held peculiar authority. This was Locke's *tabula rasa* dogma that there are no "innate" ideas and that **all knowledge is derived from experience**.

Let us then suppose the mind to be, as we say, white paper, void of all characters, without any ideas; how comes it to be furnished? Whence comes it by that vast store which the busy and boundless fancy of man has painted on it with an almost endless variety? Whence has it all the materials of reason and knowledge? To this I answer, in one word, from **experience**.

John Locke without his wig.

Locke's empirical view was aimed specifically against the Rationalism of **René Descartes** (1596–1650).

There are ideas (for instance those of God, Mind, Body, or the Triangle) whose truth may be recognized by the light of **reason alone** *and could thus be called "innate".*

Locke's empiricism distinguished two different kinds of experience: **external sensation** and **internal reflection**.

In France, Locke's philosophy was popularized by **Etienne Condillac** (1715–80), whose *Essai sur l'origine des connaissances* (1746) stressed the role of sensory impressions or sensations.

*This "sensationalism" is deemed consistent with the **materialist** and determinist view of human nature developed by other **philosophes** such as La Mettrie and d'Holbach.*

Locke himself had stressed the role of reflection and recognized the role of mental faculties. In addition, he believed in our innate tendency to seek pleasure and avoid pain. These aspects were downplayed by Condillac.

The Language of the Self

Pierre Coste, who in 1700 translated Locke's *Essay Concerning Human Understanding*, inserted a note to explain why he translated Locke's term "consciousness" by the French *conscience*. First he cites Cicero's *conscientia* ("moral awareness", "knowledge of oneself") but admits that he is "diverting" the French word *conscience* "from its ordinary sense, in order to give it one which has never been given it in [the French] Language".

*The English word is **consciousness** . . . In French we do not have, in my opinion, any words but **sentiment** & **conviction** which answer, in any significant way, to this idea.*

12

Understanding the Limits of Our Understanding

For hundreds of years, the whole territory of biography had been the special preserve of priests and confessors. The church had a richly developed language of moral principles. Locke's treatment of human understanding led to the development of a new language of interiority which we might term "psychological", a word not much used in the 18th century. Locke launched a devastating critique of the schoolman's "curious and unexplainable Web of perplexed Words" and set in motion the mapping out of a new continent of the interior.

Our understanding is limited. Let us accept its limitations. But within the limits imposed, let us make the most of our understanding, by studying it and getting to know how it operates . . . We should observe how our ideas are formed and how they combine, one with another, and how the memory retains them. Of all this activity, we have hitherto been in total ignorance.

Psychology and the Novel

Psychology, as the 18th century understood it, was the one mapped out by Locke. Locke's *Essay* is thus at the fountainhead of the sort of literature which deals in the reactions, coherent or incoherent, of the "Self" to the impressions which affect and shape it.

I OWE NOTHING TO NATURE; I OWE EVERYTHING TO A LONG AND CAREFUL STUDY OF CERTAIN GREAT BOOKS: THE OLD AND THE NEW TESTAMENTS, AND LOCKE WHOM I BEGAN TO READ IN MY YOUTH AND HAVE GONE ON READING EVER SINCE.

By the time **Laurence Sterne** (1713–68) was writing *The Life and Opinions of Tristram Shandy* (1759–67), Locke's *Essay* had infiltrated literary consciousness in a way quite unlike that of any other "philosophical" book. Sterne's novel even offers a thumbnail sketch of Locke's great *Essay*.

Tristram Shandy

Pray, Sir, in all the reading which you have ever read, did you ever read such a book as Locke's **Essay upon the Human Understanding**? Don't answer me rashly – because many, I know, quote the book, who have not read it – and many have read it who understand it not.

If either of these is your case . . .
I will tell you
in three words
what the book is.
It is a history – a history!
of whom?
what?
where?
when?

. . . It is a history-book . . . of what passes in a man's own mind; and if you will say so much of the book, and no more, believe me, you will cut no contemptible figure in a metaphysical circle.

Locke's Social Influence

Locke's influence went beyond the schools and universities, the learned societies and academies. The "ideas" of Locke had become one of the indispensable "properties" of the fashionable intelligentsia.

Fictions in the Service of Truth

In the literature of the 18th century, there is continual interplay between philosophy and fiction. These novelists were the inheritors of a tradition stretching back to the Roman Empire. But in the Age of Enlightenment, fiction faced new and urgent tasks.

The novel was uniquely suited to an age when an individual might make his or her own way in the world. An increasingly informed and curious readership awaited tales which were experimental and exemplary. Received ideas are put to the test of experience; literary conventions are measured against the imperatives of a disorderly reality.

Characteristically, the Enlightenment novel focuses on a single individual and monitors the impact of an unpredictable world on that person's experience.

IT PROVES AGAIN AND AGAIN LOCKE'S POSTULATE THAT WE ARE MADE BY WHAT HAPPENS TO US.

There is another sort of knowledge beyond the power of learning to bestow, and this is to be had by conversation . . . the true practical system can only be learnt from the world.

17

The Adventures of . . .

Our 18th century heroes and heroines travel about the world in their picaresque journeys through life – expecting to improve themselves as they improve their lot in life. At the very least, they attempt to maintain their sense of **self-worth** in the face of adversity, corruption and seduction.

In many of these novels, we come upon the main character engaged in the midst of some moral dilemma or problem. Often we learn of each move they make, each impulse they suffer, through the spontaneous letters they write.

Pamela (Samuel Richardson), **La Nouvelle Héloïse** *(Jean-Jacques Rousseau),* **Die Leiden des Jungen Werthers** *(Johann Wolfgang von Goethe) and* **Les Liaisons Dangereuses** *(Choderlos de Laclos).*

Philosophers' Novels

The novelists of the Age of Enlightenment did not simply borrow philosophical ideas, they dramatized and brought them to life. And some of the great novels of the age were written by its most important philosophers. The biggest bestseller of the 18th century was *La Nouvelle Héloïse* by **Jean-Jacques Rousseau** (1712–78). Montesquieu's *Lettres Persanes* and Voltaire's *Candide* also enjoyed European success, with enormous sales. Diderot's masterpiece was his *Jacques le Fataliste*.

BUT VOLTAIRE AND I BOTH EXCELLED AT ANOTHER FORM OF SHORT FICTION WHICH IS EVEN CLOSER TO PHILOSOPHY IN THE STRICTEST SENSE.

DIDEROT AND I PRODUCED EXAMPLES OF THE *CONTE PHILOSOPHIQUE*, OR PHILOSOPHICAL TALE, IN WHICH CHARACTER AND PLOT ARE SUBORDINATED TO THE NEED TO EXPLORE A PARTICULAR PROBLEM.

Like Defoe's *Robinson Crusoe*, but on a smaller scale, these tales are "thought experiments".

19

Voltaire's *contes* include his novella, *Candide*, and the shorter tales, *Micromegas*, *Zadig*, *The Ingenu* and *The White Bull*.

One of Voltaire's earliest biographers, the **Marquis de Condorcet** (1743–94), recognized the artistic genius that went into the making of *Candide* and other such philosophical *contes*.

"This genre has the misfortune of appearing easy; but it requires a rare talent, that of knowing how to express by a play of wit and of imagination, or even by the very events of the story, the results of a profound philosophy without ceasing to be natural and how to be pungent without ceasing to be true. One has to be a philosopher, yet not seem to be one." Condorcet

Candide

In his novel *Candide, or Optimism* (1759), Voltaire satirized not only optimism but all forms of system, from Leibniz's metaphysical one to the colonial and Church systems, and indeed the system of logic itself. The novel follows the hero, Candide, through most of the then-known world, exposing the hypocrisies and madness of its institutions and attitudes. Candide is accompanied by Dr Pangloss who parrots an illogical travesty of Leibniz's system. He is unshakeable in his faith that logic and reason can somehow explain away all the chaotic wretchedness of existence by grandly, metaphysically, ignoring the facts. The novel ends only when Candide has finally grasped that work is more profitable than vain speculation.

Pangloss taught metaphysico-theologico-cosmo-codology. He could prove wonderfully that there is no effect without cause . . . in this best of all possible worlds.

ALL IS WELL . . . OBSERVE HOW NOSES WERE MADE TO BEAR SPECTACLES, AND SO WE HAVE SPECTACLES.

WE MUST CULTIVATE OUR GARDEN.

21

Novels of the Enlightenment

Daniel Defoe (1660–1731) was one of the first to earn his living by freelance writing. His more than 500 published works include political and religious journalism. In 1704, while employed as a government agent, he started his own newspaper, *The Review*. Journalism is the basis for some major works like *A Journal of the Plague Year* (1722). Defoe was nearly 60 when he wrote his first work of fiction, *Robinson Crusoe* (1719), followed by others, including *The Fortunes and Misfortunes of the Famous Moll Flanders* (1722) and *Roxana, the Fortunate Mistress* (1724). In 1707, **Jonathan Swift** (1667–1745) was sent to London as an envoy of the Irish Church. He wrote numerous pamphlets and founded the Scriblerus Club with other satirists, such as the inventor of the figure of "John Bull", **John Arbuthnot** (1667–1735), the poet **Alexander Pope** (1688–1744) and the playwright **John Gay** (1685–1732). In 1726 Swift published his great satire, *Gulliver's Travels*. The novels of **Samuel Richardson** (1689–1761) were meant to enforce a moral in a new form which he called "writing to the moment". *Pamela, or Virtue Rewarded* (1740) and *Clarissa, or the History of a Young Lady* (1747–8), are made up of letters supposed to have been written immediately after the event by the people involved. This technique of the epistolary novel was satirized by **Henry Fielding** (1707–54) in his *Shamela* (1741). Fielding's satirical plays provoked the passage of the Licensing Act (1737) and censorship of the stage. In his preface to *Joseph Andrews* (1742), Fielding professed himself at a loss as to what to call his form of fiction – a "comic epic poem, in prose". His other major novels are *Jonathan Wild* (1743) and *Tom Jones* (1749). Fielding's example was followed by the Scottish novelist **Tobias Smollett** (1721–71), whose novels include *Roderick Random* (1748), *Peregrine Pickle* (1751), *The Adventures of Sir Launcelot Greaves* (1762), and *The Expedition of Humphry Clinker* (1771). In 1749, **John Cleland** (1709–89) adapted the formulae of the novel to present *The Memoirs of a Woman of Pleasure* (usually known as *Fanny Hill*), and created a pornographic classic.

In desperate need of some ready money to support his ailing mother, **Samuel Johnson** (1709–84) took just two weeks to write *The History of Rasselas, Prince of Abissinia* (1759), a moral tale which closely parallels Voltaire's *Candide*, published in the same year. An English clergyman, **Laurence Sterne** (1713–68), produced the most extraordinary novel of the Enlightenment, *The Life and Opinions of Tristram Shandy* (in 9 volumes, 1759–67). His other major work, *A Sentimental Journey* (1768), was representative of the literature of "sensibility" which gained ground in the later half of the 18th century.

Abbé Prevost (1697–1763) was an enthusiastic journalist and a tireless translator who frequented the circle of *philosophes*. His popular novel *Manon Lescaut* (1731) introduced a genuinely tragic element into the genre. **Pierre Carlet de Marivaux** (1688–1763), the leading French playwright of the 18th century, also wrote *La Vie de Marianne* (1731–2) and *Le Paysan parvenu* (1734–5), fine, though unfinished, novels which captured life in contemporary France. Montesquieu's *Persian Letters* (1721) was the century's bestseller until Voltaire's *Candide* (1759), which he published simultaneously in Paris, Geneva, Amsterdam, London and Brussels to make censorship impossible. An English translation came out within six weeks. Diderot's serious fictions include *The Nun* (1760), *Rameau's Nephew* (1763) and his masterwork, *Jacques the Fatalist and His Master* (15 instalments, 1778–80). Diderot often incorporated real events and people into fictional philosophical dialogues, such as *D'Alembert's Dream* (1769). The bestselling work of fiction in late 18th century France was Rousseau's *Julie, or The New Héloïse* (1761), an epistolary novel about the tribulations of frustrated love, which encouraged the fashion for sentimentality and excited "sensibility". *Dangerous Liaisons* (1782) by **Pierre-Ambroise-François Choderlos de Laclos** (1741–1803) tells the story of two unscrupulous seducers in subtle letters full of irony. *The New Justine* (1797), a novel by the **Marquis de Sade** (1740–1814), is a revised and expanded version of his *Justine, or the Misfortunes of Virtue* (1779), a detailed expression of sexual sadism, and was meant to evoke echoes of Rousseau's title.

The Idea of the Noble Savage

The 18th century was a great time of tourism, marine trade and exploration which encouraged a form of "comparative anthropology".

In 1767, the French explorer **Louis Antoine de Bougainville** (1729–1811) arrived in Tahiti. In 1769, **Captain Cook** (1728–79) stayed there four months to observe the transit of Venus. Bougainville, as a follower of Rousseau, found in the Tahitians all the qualities of the "noble savage". Captain Cook was a hard-headed Yorkshireman.

Diderot's *Supplement to Bougainville's Voyage* used the perspective of the "innocent eye" of the Tahitian to highlight the strangeness of customs and manners considered "normal". Soon the brightest wits of Paris and London were beginning to ask whether the word "civilization" was not more appropriate to the uncorrupted islanders of the South Seas than to the exceptionally corrupt society of 18th century Europe.

This idea of the noble savage (or simple folk) took root in the literature of the 18th century. Hardly an author, witty or serious, failed to describe his "savage" to his readers. Montesquieu began with his Persian prince, as we shall see; Voltaire immortalized the type in Candide; Buffon analyzed him in his awakening of Adam; Rousseau created his own role by playing the savage in solitary retirement.

By about 1770, there was not a philosophical apprentice who did not seek to revise the laws and customs of his country with the advice of his Chinese or Iroquois, just as the son of a good family might travel with his priest. Let's see how Montesquieu proceeded with the idea.

The Persian Letters

Montesquieu (1689–1755), or, to give him his full name, Charles-Louis de Secondat, Baron de la Brède et de Montesquieu, was born into the magistrature or *noblesse de robe*, and inherited a position as president of the Bordeaux *parlement*. In 1721 he published (anonymously in Holland) what was to become one of the most influential anti-Establishment works of the 18th century, the *Lettres Persanes* (*Persian Letters*).

The book consists of a series of letters written by two Persians, Usbek and Ricca, during their residence in Paris, and their travels in Europe, to a variety of correspondents at home. The Persians have set out on their version of the Grand Tour.

OUR PURPOSE IS TO EDUCATE OURSELVES ABOUT THE CUSTOMS AND SOCIAL ARRANGEMENTS IN THE WEST.

RICCA AND I ARE PERHAPS THE FIRST PERSIANS TO HAVE LEFT OUR COUNTRY SOLELY FOR LOVE OF KNOWLEDGE. WE HAVE ABANDONED THE ATTRACTIONS OF A QUIET LIFE – AS WELL AS OUR MANY WIVES – IN ORDER TO PURSUE THE LABORIOUS SEARCH FOR WISDOM.

In 1754 Montesquieu offered "Some Reflections on the Persian Letters" in which he explains that ". . . in ordinary novels, digressions are permissible only when they themselves form a new story . . . But in using *the letter form*, in which neither the choice of characters, nor the subjects discussed, have to fit in with any preconceived intentions or plans, the author has taken advantage of the fact that he can include philosophy, politics, and moral discourse with the novel, and can connect everything together with a secret chain which remains, as it were, invisible."

*Nothing pleased the public more, in the **Persian Letters**, than to find unexpectedly a sort of novel.*

Many of the letters describe the people and institutions in France. To the eyes of the Persian visitors, some of the accepted customs seem very strange indeed. Naive but open-minded, they are constantly trying to distinguish what is local and conventional from what is universal or "natural". For example, in *Letter 30*, Ricca writes to Ibben about the way that Parisiennes react to clothes and costume as conventional signs. "When I arrived, they looked at me as though I had been sent from Heaven: old men and young, women and children, they all wanted to see me. In a word, never was a man *seen* as much as I was."

This made me decide to give up Persian costume and dress like a European. The experiment made me realize what I was really worth. Free of all foreign adornments, I found myself assessed more exactly. I had reason to complain of my tailor, who, from one instant to the next, had made me lose the esteem and attention of the public; for all at once I fell into a terrible state of non-existence.

Montesquieu was able to make fun of the pillars of the Establishment, such as the church hierarchy.

"The Pope is the chief of the Christians; he is an ancient idol, worshipped now from habit. Once he was formidable even to princes, for he would depose them as easily as our magnificent sultans depose the kings of Iremetia or Georgia. But nobody fears him any longer . . . Bishops, when assembled together, compose articles of belief. When they are on their own, virtually their only function is to dispense people from obedience to the Christian Law." *Letter 29*, Ricca to Ibben at Smyrna

I HAVE HEARD THAT IN SPAIN AND PORTUGAL THERE ARE CERTAIN DERVISHES WHO CANNOT SEE A JOKE, AND WHO BURN A MAN AS THEY WOULD STRAW.

When the ecclesiastical authorities expressed their outrage, Montesquieu was able to say that the Persians simply displayed their ignorance.

29

"Moreover, this king is a great magician. He exerts authority even over the minds of his subjects; he makes them think what he wants. If there are only a million crowns in the exchequer, and he needs two million, all he needs to do is persuade them that one crown is worth two, and they believe it." *Letter 24, Ricca to Ibben at Smyrna*

If he is involved in a difficult war without any money, all he has to do is to get it into their heads that a piece of paper will do for money, and they are immediately convinced of it.

What particularly excited readers was the combination of the erotic and the exotic in the unfolding story of the unruly harem which the Persian traveller has left behind. In an early letter, Usbek's chief eunuch laments his fate, and one of Usbek's wives bemoans his absence.

I remember those happy times when you used to come to my arms . . . How wretched a woman is, having such violent desires, when she is deprived of the only man who can appease them; when, left to herself, she must spend her time in a frenzy of unsatisfied desire.

The *Persian Letters* is also a steamy novel of frustrated sexual passions. As the Persian *philosophes* continue their travels, they contrast sexual taboos and mores in the West with their own. Unfortunately, the longer the Persian travellers stay away, the more disorder increases in the Eastern *seraglio*.

Montesquieu clearly sees the harem as a form of despotism, and as such unnatural. It corrupts all of its agents. The eunuchs seek compensation for their sexual deprivation by gratifying a lust for power. After she has poisoned herself in despair, Roxane, the favourite wife of Usbek, writes in her final letter that she has deceived her tyrant husband.

I HAVE CORRECTED YOUR LAWS *IN ACCORDANCE WITH THE LAWS OF NATURE.*

Montesquieu's novel sold like hot cakes. There were ten editions within a year. Montesquieu, who had married in 1717, enjoyed considerable social and amorous success.

I FOLLOWED THE EXAMPLE OF USBEK AND RICCA AND TRAVELLED AROUND EUROPE, INCLUDING ENGLAND.

In 1726 he sold his *parlement* position and decided to dedicate himself to more serious writing. In 1748, after struggling with blindness and financial difficulties, he published one of the most influential political works of the 18th century, *The Spirit of the Laws*. But more of that later.

Voltaire Flees to England

François-Marie Arouet (1694–1778), who later took the name **Voltaire**, was born a commoner in Paris and educated by the Jesuits. He enjoyed early literary successes with his version of the *Oedipus* tragedy and the epic *La Henriade* which retold the legends of Henry IV, France's tolerant king. These earned Voltaire pensions from Louis XV, from the queen and the Duc d'Orléans. But Voltaire was also notorious for satirical poems and lampoons of all kinds, and he spent nearly a year in the Bastille in 1717.

Voltaire was impudent enough to challenge an aristocrat, the Chevalier de Rohan, to a duel.

FEELING THAT SUCH AN ENCOUNTER WAS BENEATH HIM, THE CHEVALIER SENT HIS SERVANTS TO BEAT ME UP. MY APPEALS FOR FAIR PLAY FELL ON DEAF EARS. THE CHEVALIER'S ARISTOCRATIC FRIENDS CLOSED RANKS.

This persuaded Voltaire that it was necessary to flee the country. In May 1726, he landed in England to start two and a half years of self-imposed exile.

Letters on England

The *Persian Letters* had offered only a light-hearted and indirect attack on the institutions and conventions of French society. Its many aristocratic readers treated it as a series of "in-jokes". Montesquieu, after all, was "one of them". Voltaire instead was a commoner who wrote of his own observations as a traveller and exile. His *Letters Concerning the English Nation*, first published in England in 1733, appeared in France as *Lettres Philosophiques* (*Philosophical Letters*) the following year.

I used the English model to attack the French system, French failings and abuses. In particular, I was struck by the extent of religious toleration in England, the liberalism of English politics and commerce and the vigour of science and philosophy in England.

Voltaire's *Letters* have been described as "the first bomb hurled against the Ancien Régime". Surreptitious editions of the book appeared in France. Voltaire's arrest was ordered. The book was officially burned and its sale absolutely forbidden.

Voltaire on Religion in England

Voltaire's book on the English begins with four letters "On the Quakers". He was attracted by their simple, undogmatic ethos and their practical embodiment of spiritual and moral values. Although he pokes gentle fun at them, Voltaire was clearly deeply impressed by the fact that the Quaker faith was not dominated by a priesthood.

SO YOU HAVE NO PRIESTS?

NO, MY FRIEND, AND WE ARE ALL THE BETTER FOR IT. GOD FORBID THAT WE SHOULD DARE TO ORDER SOMEBODY TO RECEIVE THE HOLY SPIRIT ON SUNDAY TO THE EXCLUSION OF THE REST OF THE FAITHFUL.

Voltaire devotes a letter each to the Anglicans, the Presbyterians and other smaller religious sects. Throughout his life, Voltaire remained a tireless opponent of the Catholic Church's intolerance. But this does not mean that he was himself indifferent to religion. On the contrary, he was haunted by religion all his life.

IF GOD DID NOT EXIST, HE WOULD HAVE TO BE INVENTED.

Freedom of Conscience and the Commercial Spirit

Voltaire's stay in England was interrupted briefly while he dashed back to France to take care of his business affairs. Always a shrewd businessman and speculator, Voltaire was able to make enough money from his business ventures to ensure his intellectual independence and to finance a glittering lifestyle. "Commerce, which has enriched English citizens, has helped to make them free, and this freedom in its turn has extended commerce, and that has made the greatness of the nation."

Go into the London Stock Exchange, a place of more dignity than many royal courts, and you will find representatives of all nations assembled there to promote human welfare; there a Jew, the Mahometan and the Christian deal with one another as though they were of the same religion; the only persons whom they count as infidels are those who go bankrupt . . .

On Parliament

"The English nation is the only one on earth which has succeeded in controlling the power of kings by resisting them, which by effort after effort has at last established this wise system of government in which the prince, all-powerful for doing good, has his hands tied for doing evil, in which the aristocrats are great without arrogance or vassals, and in which the people share in the government without confusion."

Voltaire pokes fun at the antics in the House of Commons, and at other shortcomings in the practice of English politics, but he also makes clear his admiration for the English political system with its limited constitutional monarchy.

England had gradually developed towards equality before the law, and a system of taxation from which nobody would be exempt. (Decades later, the tax exemption of the aristocracy and the higher clergy was a scandal which inflamed the French Revolution.)

A man is by no means exempt from paying certain taxes here simply because he is an aristocrat or because he is a priest . . . You will hear nothing here about high, middle or low justice.

"Not long ago, Mr Shipping began his speech in the House of Commons with these words: 'The majesty of the English people would be hurt, etc.' The strangeness of the expression caused a loud burst of laughter but, by no means disconcerted, he repeated the same words in a firm tone, and there was no more laughing."

The Patron Saints of the Enlightenment

The patron saints of the Enlightenment were three Englishmen: Bacon, Locke and Newton. The most serious and technical of Voltaire's *Letters* were devoted to these three, and d'Alembert and Diderot dedicated the *Encyclopédie* to them.

In 1789, **Thomas Jefferson** (1743–1826), the principal author of the Declaration of Independence, ordered for his library a composite portrait of the same three Englishmen.

They have laid the foundation for the physical and moral sciences of modernity . . . The three greatest men that ever lived, without any exception.

Montesquieu and Voltaire were the pupils and followers of England's philosophers and great men. Without the English, reason and philosophy would still be in the most despicable infancy in France.

41

The Father of Experimental Philosophy

Locke's great predecessor in the empirical tradition was **Francis Bacon** (1561–1626), the English statesman and philosopher, widely acknowledged as the "father of experimental philosophy".

*I advocated a great reform of knowledge based on **direct observation**, rejecting the blind worship of authorities in favour of the immediate world of **sense experience**.*

Bacon represented the divisions of knowledge as the branches of a tree. The main branches of this "tree of knowledge" were derived from the three main faculties of the mind: **memory**, **imagination** and **reason**.

Memory – the source of historical knowledge
Imagination – the source of poetry
Reason – the source of philosophy

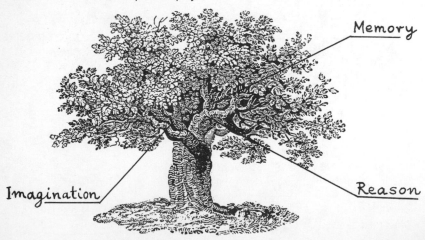

John Locke's Politics

Locke's influence extended beyond philosophy. His writings on politics also inspired Enlightenment reformers like Diderot, Jefferson and others. Locke returned to England from exile in Holland with the manuscripts of his *Two Treatises of Government* and the *Essay Concerning Human Understanding*, both published in 1690.

*The **consent of the people** is the sole basis of a government's authority. Governments have **no other** duties beyond those for which they were first instituted: the preservation of life, liberty and property.*

Locke suggested that should the prince (or "single hereditary Person") use his power in an arbitrary way, without the consent of the people, then "the people are at liberty to provide for themselves". Rebellion was justified to counter the arbitrary or despotic use of power by a ruler.

Isaac Newton

The scientific achievements of **Sir Isaac Newton** (1642–1727) were colossal. Calculus – differential and integral – was a powerful new mathematical tool developed independently by Newton and by **Gottfried Wilhelm von Leibniz** (1646–1716). Newton's masterpiece, the *Mathematical Principles of Natural Philosophy* (or *Principia Mathematica*, 1687) defined a new science of dynamics, reconciling Kepler's treatment of planetary motion with Galileo's treatment of terrestrial motion.

I provided elegant mathematical descriptions of the order of the cosmos and the motion of the planets. I proposed a law of universal gravitation and suggested that planetary space was infinite.

In 1704, Newton's second great book, *Opticks*, set out his conclusions about the nature of light. It closed with a set of speculations and queries which inspired scientific investigation throughout the 18th century.

Newton for Beginners

Newton's work attracted a host of popularizers, including Voltaire, not only in the *Letters* of 1733 but in *Éléments de la Physique de Newton* (*Elements of Newtonian Physics*), which appeared in 1738.

MY MISTRESS, THE MARQUISE EMILIE DU CHÂTELET, TRANSLATED NEWTON INTO FRENCH.

Many of these popular accounts depicted a universe that was more mechanistic than Newton himself would have liked. They suggested that Newton had described the *whole* of the created universe as an ordered, self-regulating system.

The beauty of Newton's mathematical formulae, Laws of Motion and so on, apparently offered a simpler view of the universe than Newton really intended.

In fact, **gravitation** was itself a fairly mysterious force.

Entropy was identified by Newton as characteristic of closed systems. (Entropy: the tendency of a closed system to run down, to lose all energy, and hence organization.)

Newton himself felt that he had shown the necessity of a First Cause, and became more and more involved in alchemy and other researches which we would today regard as "mystical".

I seem to have been only as a boy playing on the sea-shore, and diverting myself in now and then finding a smoother pebble or a prettier shell than ordinary, whilst the great ocean of truth lay all undiscovered before me.

Newton, the Paradigm

Newton's achievements so far advanced the cause of physics and the natural sciences that in most other areas of knowledge writers tried to generalize his example. Newton was taken to be the **paradigm**, or model, of a true scientist.

Shortly after Newton's death, J.T. Desaguliers, whose popularizations of Newton had wide circulation, foretold the broadest possible application of Newton's methods in a poem entitled *The Newtonian System of the World, the Best Model of Government*. Voltaire hoped that there might one day be a transfer of the methods of the natural sciences to history.

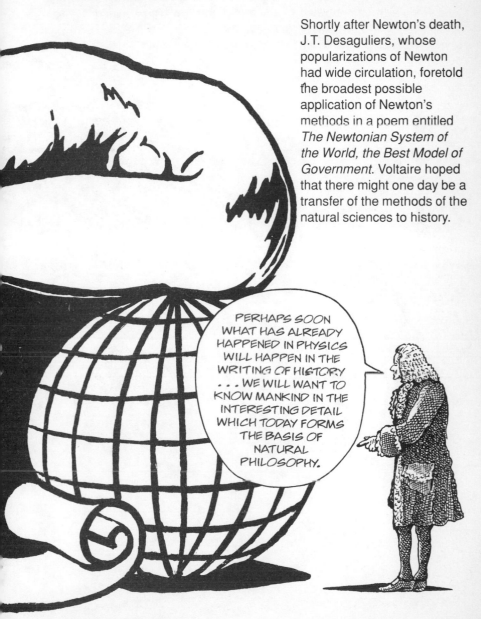

PERHAPS SOON WHAT HAS ALREADY HAPPENED IN PHYSICS WILL HAPPEN IN THE WRITING OF HISTORY . . . WE WILL WANT TO KNOW MANKIND IN THE INTERESTING DETAIL WHICH TODAY FORMS THE BASIS OF NATURAL PHILOSOPHY.

The *Philosophes*

Montesquieu, Voltaire, Diderot, Rousseau, Buffon, Condillac, Turgot, Condorcet, d'Alembert, Morellet, d'Holbach, Helvétius, Grimm and Raynal.

With the example of Montesquieu and Voltaire set before them, the men who made up the "republic of letters" began to show a new self-confidence and militancy. In Paris, with its cafés and clubs, its journals and booksellers, a new breed was emerging: the *philosophe*.

The *philosophes* were intellectuals, men of letters, but not professional philosophers, and certainly not ivory tower academics. The Parisian atmosphere of ideas, disputes, discussion and conflict produced an Enlightenment élite. It was here that the militant wing of the Enlightenment was concentrated: thinking, writing, polemicizing and fighting – amongst themselves and with the world.

The *philosophes* were the priests, soldiers, and propagandists of the new spirit of reason, tolerance and progress. Voltaire issued rallying calls, urging them to unite.

But the true organizing genius of the movement was the son of a provincial cutler, **Denis Diderot** (1713–84), who united scores of the more radical intellects of the time in the creation of that most characteristic product of the Enlightenment, the *Encyclopédie*.

The enemies of this new radicalism reacted with anger and suspicion. "Just what is a *philosophe*?", asked the Abbé Molinier.

A kind of monster in society who feels under no obligation towards its manners and morals, its proprieties, its politics or its religion. One may expect anything from men of their ilk.

The *Encyclopédie* explained what a *philosophe* was.

One who, trampling on prejudice, tradition, universal consent, authority – in a word, all that enslaves most minds – dares to think for himself, to go back and search for the clearest general principles, to admit nothing except on the testimony of his experience and his reason.

Enlightened Woman

The *philosophes* were a brotherhood, a sociable bunch of blokes. In the clubs and coffee-houses of Britain, ladies were more or less excluded (although whores seem never to have been very far away). In France, the main meeting places of the *philosophes* were the *salons*.

It was an institution as essential to patronage as it was to sexual passion, in an age in which the intellectual and sexual passions were divorced from the individual's private domestic domain.

Social and intellectual life in France was much less of an all-male affair, but thinking was still largely a job for the boys. Diderot paid tribute to the role of women as interlocutors ("good listeners") in shaping the intellectual conventions of the age.

Salons were held at the homes of the *philosophes* Baron d'Holbach and Helvétius. All the other Paris *salons* were run by women, including Mme du Deffand, Mme Geoffrin, Mlle de l'Espinasse and Mme Necker. It took a great deal of skill and tact to run a *salon* successfully, and to gain the respect of temperamental intellectuals and authors. The little army of *Encyclopédistes* first grouped themselves at Mme Geoffrin's.

Enlightened Mistresses

Playing hostess to one of the *salons* was not the only way in which a woman could be actively involved in the intellectual ferment of the day. Amongst the mistresses of the leading thinkers were some truly remarkable women.

Mme d'Epinay (1726–83) was small, vivid and fragile-looking, with great lustrous eyes. She captivated Voltaire and Diderot and for many years she was the lover of **Friedrich Melchior von Grimm** (1723–1807). She was also fascinated by Rousseau, though well aware of his prickliness.

IN *1756*, I ALLOWED HIM TO RETIRE TO THE SECLUSION OF AN ISOLATED COTTAGE, KNOWN AS THE HERMITAGE, ON MY ESTATE.

Mme d'Epinay was a prolific contributor to Grimm's journal, *Correspondance Littéraire*, providing essays, theatre and book reviews, articles on politics, economics and philosophy, as well as light verse. During Grimm's travels, she and Diderot were left in charge of it. In her *Memoirs de Mme de Montbrillant*, she assembled a brilliant *pastiche* of dinner-party conversations which represented the ideas and opinions, and sometimes the actual words, of the *philosophes*.

Voltaire's companion of many years was the **Marquise Emilie du Châtelet** (1706–49). They met in 1733 when Voltaire was 39 and she was 27. She had been married for eight years and was the mother of three children. She became a very learned and accomplished woman.

Mme du Châtelet not only translated Newton into French and worked with Voltaire, but also quite independently wrote essays on scientific subjects.

DESPITE VOLTAIRE'S VAGUE DISAPPROVAL, I STUDIED THE PHILOSOPHY OF LEIBNIZ AND PRODUCED A BOOK EXPOUNDING HIS VIEW OF THE WORLD AS INTERPRETED BY HIS FOLLOWER *CHRISTIAN WOLFF.*

EVERYBODY UNDERSTANDS THE MONADS SINCE THE LEIBNIZIANS MADE THE BRILLIANT ACQUISITION OF MME DU CHÂTELET.

IT IS DEPLORABLE THAT A FRENCHWOMAN SUCH AS MME DU CHÂTELET SHOULD USE HER INTELLIGENCE TO EMBROIDER SUCH SPIDERS' WEBS AND MAKE THESE HERESIES ATTRACTIVE.

At the age of 43 she acquired a new lover, the 27-year-old Marquis de Saint-Lambert, by whom she became pregnant. Despite being nursed by Voltaire, she died shortly after the birth. Voltaire was inconsolable. "I have lost one who was my friend for 25 years, a great man, whose only defect was being a woman."

Readers and Censors

For whom did the *philosophes* write? In the first instance, they wrote for their fellow *philosophes* in the international network. But they also campaigned to spread their lights among a growing public of readers.

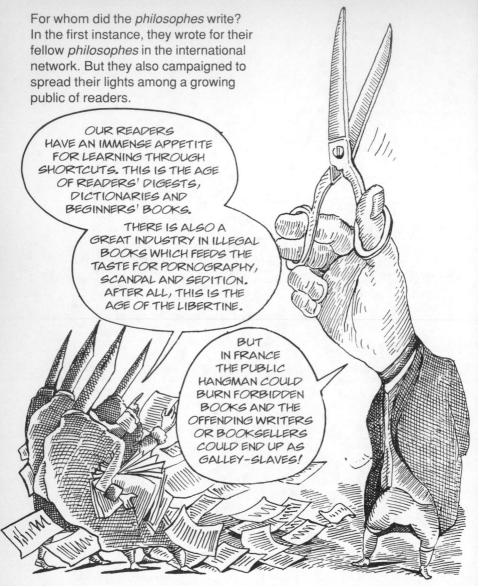

OUR READERS HAVE AN IMMENSE APPETITE FOR LEARNING THROUGH SHORTCUTS. THIS IS THE AGE OF READERS' DIGESTS, DICTIONARIES AND BEGINNERS' BOOKS.

THERE IS ALSO A GREAT INDUSTRY IN ILLEGAL BOOKS WHICH FEEDS THE TASTE FOR PORNOGRAPHY, SCANDAL AND SEDITION. AFTER ALL, THIS IS THE AGE OF THE LIBERTINE.

BUT IN FRANCE THE PUBLIC HANGMAN COULD BURN FORBIDDEN BOOKS AND THE OFFENDING WRITERS OR BOOKSELLERS COULD END UP AS GALLEY-SLAVES!

Censorship, absent from England and Holland, remained a dangerous fact of intellectual life in the rest of Europe. Publication (usually by booksellers) required legal permission from a court minister. Magistrates in France, however, soon learned that burning books only promoted sales, so they preferred to impound books and imprison booksellers with as little fuss as possible.

Industry and Science

Practical innovations in industrial technology were often provided by engineers associated with the Scottish Enlightenment, such as **James Watt** (1736–1819) who devised an efficient steam engine and the unit "horsepower". The age of the machine began with the alliance of steam power and the iron foundries in the coalfields of Derbyshire, which put Britain at the centre of the Industrial Revolution.

WE ARE THE WORKSHOP OF THE WORLD!

Educated readers grasped the importance of scientific experiment – putting ideas to the test of experience. But over-confidence in science led even the wisest to imagine that it would soon progress to an end in absolute certainty. In many ways, the 18th century was alarmingly gullible, an age of visionaries, pseudo-scientists and quacks like **Franz Mesmer** (1734–1815), who claimed to cure diseases by the power of "animal magnetism".

The *Encyclopédie*

The most characteristic product and impressive monument of the Enlightenment was the *Encyclopédie*. This was originally commissioned as a translation and revision of Ephraim Chambers' *Cyclopaedia*, first published in Edinburgh in 1727.

After the first editor had given up, the project was finally successfully launched by Denis Diderot and **Jean Le Rond d'Alembert** (1717–83).

THE *ENCYCLOPÉDIE* EXPANDED TO ITS EVENTUAL 28 FOLIO VOLUMES.

AND IT BECAME A POLEMICAL WORK DESIGNED TO EDUCATE AND CHANGE PUBLIC OPINION.

Volume I of the *Encyclopédie, ou Dictionnaire Raisonné des Sciences, des Arts et des Métiers (Encyclopedia, or Analytical Dictionary of the Sciences, Arts and Crafts)* appeared in 1751. It took more than 20 years to bring the work to completion. It eventually consisted of approximately 72,000 entries and 2,500 engravings.

Because of his reputation as a mathematician, d'Alembert's name was widely respected – but it was always Diderot who did most of the work. Diderot succeeded in gathering around him an impressive array of collaborators, including among the many *philosophes*: Montesquieu, Voltaire, Charles Duclos, Rousseau, Samuel Foremy, d'Holbach, Morellet, André Théophile de Bordeu, Jacques de Vaucanson.

FATE, BUT EVEN MORE, LIFE'S NECESSITIES DO WITH US WHAT THEY WILL; WHO IS MORE AWARE OF THIS THAN I? THAT IS WHY, FOR SOME THIRTY YEARS, I HAVE, AGAINST MY INCLINATION, DEVOTED MYSELF TO THE *ENCYCLOPÉDIE*, WHILE WRITING BUT TWO PLAYS.

Later he was ably assisted by a new convert to the cause, the indefatigable **Chevalier de Jaucourt** (1704–99), who, like Diderot, wrote hundreds of articles and supervised the work of an army of hack writers engaged in compilation.

The Tree of Knowledge

In his "Preliminary Discourse" to the *Encyclopédie*, d'Alembert claimed to offer readers an overview of all the various branches of knowledge and their relation to one another in the form of a genealogical tree. He based it on diagrams offered by Bacon and adapted in Chambers' *Cyclopaedia*.

LIKE BACON, I SUGGEST THAT THE VARIOUS BRANCHES OF KNOWLEDGE ARE DIRECTLY RELATED TO THE DIFFERENT FACULTIES OF THE MIND.

But there is little room for anything that could not reach reason through the senses. The traditional doctrines of the church were relegated to a very minor branch of the tree of knowledge.

Who Are the "Great Men" of History?

Citing "Chancellor Bacon" as his authority, d'Alembert offers a potted view of history in which the "Great Men" are not kings and conquerors, but scholars and philosophers.

D'Alembert gives a short account of the greatest of the great: Bacon, Descartes, Newton and Locke. But he offers also a shortlist of the leading scientists and philosophers, including Galileo, Harvey, Huyghens, Pascal, Fontenelle, Buffon, Condillac, Voltaire, Montesquieu and Rousseau.

THE TRIUMPHAL ADVANCE OF ENLIGHTENMENT SWEEPS RIGHT UP TO THE PRESENT, THAT IS, UP TO THE *ENCYCLOPÉDIE* ITSELF.

Galileo Buffon Pascal Montesquieu Fontenelle Condillac Voltaire Rousseau

"The *Discours préliminaire* abounds in violent and heroic metaphors: the breaking of chains, the rending of veils, the clashing of doctrines, the storming of citadels . . . the *philosophes* [are cast] in a heroic role. Persecuted or disdained, they battled alone, fighting for future generations who would grant them the recognition that their contemporaries had refused." Robert Darnton, *Philosophers Trim The Tree of Knowledge*

The Importance of Crafts or Trades

One of the ways in which the *Encyclopédie* exerted great influence was signalled in the last word of its title: *métiers*. The *Encyclopédie* set out to do full justice not only to the arts and sciences, but also to the crafts and skills of tradespeople and master craftsmen.

Diderot, the son of a master cutler, was himself largely responsible for this component of the project. He travelled about France to interview master craftsmen about their trades and to learn their method.

I PERSUADED SOME OF THEM TO RE-ASSEMBLE THEIR EQUIPMENT FOR ME IN PARIS, SO THAT METICULOUS DRAWINGS COULD BE MADE FOR THE MANY VOLUMES OF PLATES.

In his article on heraldry, that most aristocratic of obsessions, the nobleman Chevalier de Jaucourt remarked: "There does not exist a single pamphlet on the art of making shirts, stockings, shoes, bread; the *Encyclopédie* is the first and unique work describing these arts useful to men, while the book trade is inundated with books on the vain and ridiculous science of armorial bearings."

Metaphysics and Machinery

The traditional distinction between the "liberal" and the "mechanical" arts had the unfortunate effect of degrading people who were very estimable and very useful. As Diderot remarked: "How strangely we judge! We demand that people should be usefully engaged, and we disdain useful men."

Diderot compared the workings of a complicated machine to a complex metaphysical system, and drew attention to the way in which human experience and knowledge were sedimented in practical machinery.

In what physical or metaphysical system do we find more intelligence, discernment, and consistency than in the machines for drawing gold or making stockings, and in the frames of the braid-makers, the gauze-makers, the drapers, or the silk workers?

The Pinnacle of Success

The expensive volumes of the *Encyclopédie* were of immense fascination to polite society. Voltaire invented a tale to illustrate the impact of the *Encyclopédie* on the aristocracy and even the king himself.

"One night Louis XV was having supper at the Trianon with some intimate friends. The talk turned upon game-shooting and then upon gunpowder."

"No matter; the thing was soon remedied. At a sign, the footmen hurried away to fetch the *Encyclopédie* . . ."

"There, under 'powder', 'rouge' and 'silk-weaving', was all they needed to know. Soon they had all pounced on the volumes of the *Encyclopédie* . . . and in no time they found what they wanted. People who contemplated going to law found exactly where they stood legally. The king got to know all about his regal prerogatives. While they were all thus busily turning the pages, the Comte de C— said in a voice loud enough for all to hear . . ."

Sire, you are indeed fortunate to have, in your reign, men capable of mastering all the arts, and of handing on their knowledge to posterity. Everything is here, from the way to manufacture a pin, to that of casting and firing your big guns. Everything, from the infinitely small to the infinitely great . . .

The *Philosophes* Under Attack

The *Encyclopédie* was not universally welcomed. The group of *philosophes* involved in the project attracted fierce opposition. Critics such as Elie Fréron, Charles Palissot and Jacob-Nicolas Moreau wrote articles and satires, and the Jesuits accused the *Encyclopédistes* of plagiarism. In 1752, after publication of the first two volumes of the *Encyclopédie*, the king was persuaded to order its suppression.

In 1757, the journalist Fréron denounced Diderot to the chief censor, Malesherbes.

. . . THE RINGLEADER OF A LARGE COMPANY – HE IS AT THE HEAD OF A NUMEROUS SOCIETY WHICH PULLULATES, AND MULTIPLIES ITSELF EVERY DAY BY MEANS OF INTRIGUES.

In 1760, Palissot wrote a comedy entitled *Les Philosophes* in which he lampooned Rousseau as an ape-like savage, and brutally satirized Helvétius, Diderot and Duclos.

. . . AN UNPRINCIPLED GANG OF HYPOCRITES WHO EXPLOIT THE IDLE AND GULLIBLE SOCIETY LADIES AND PROMOTE PRETENTIOUS SCHEMES.

The Crisis of 1758

The cliqueishness of *philosophes* was bound to be most pronounced when they were truly under threat.

In 1758, d'Alembert contributed an article on Geneva in which he suggested that this thriving Swiss city-state would do well to lift the ban on theatre within its walls. He seemed to go further and question the orthodoxy of the city theologians, and a furore ensued. The *parlement* of Paris outlawed the *Encyclopédie*.

"The tempest that burst over Helvétius's *De l'esprit* in 1758 and the prohibition issued against Diderot's *Encyclopédie* in the following year did more to weld the *philosophes* into a party than Voltaire's most hysterical calls for unity. Critics trying to destroy the movement only strengthened it." Peter Gay

Malesherbes – or "Monsieur Guillaume"

The *Encyclopédistes* were extremely fortunate that at this moment of crisis which threatened their whole enterprise, a friend of theirs, Malesherbes, had just been put in charge of censorship by his father, the new Chancellor of France. **Chrétien-Guillaume Lamoignon de Malesherbes** (1721–94) went on to have a long and distinguished career as a liberal statesman, as courageous as he was enlightened.

WITHOUT MALESHERBES, THE *ENCYCLOPÉDIE* WOULD MOST LIKELY NEVER HAVE DARED TO APPEAR!

FOR A TIME, I OCCUPIED A KEY POSITION IN FRANCE'S ELABORATE CENSORSHIP APPARATUS – AND I BELIEVED PASSIONATELY IN THE FREEDOM OF THE PRESS.

On many an occasion, Malesherbes gave Diderot and d'Alembert protection from behind the scenes. When in 1752 a royal decree placed a ban on the first two volumes, and an order went out to seize all the unpublished texts and plates, Malesherbes invited Diderot to hide his manuscripts in the safest of all places – Malesherbes' own house.

For and Against the King

When the king stripped the Paris *parlement* of its judicial powers in 1771 and appointed instead his own "superior councils", it fell to Malesherbes to issue a "remonstrance" calling for "an assembly of the nation" to be summoned. In the closing years of the Ancien Régime, as a result of his principled role in encouraging reform, "Monsieur Guillaume" became one of the best-loved men in France.

But even as Master of the Royal Household, he continued to wear down-at-heel clothes in deliberate defiance of Versailles etiquette. Too eager for economy and reform to suit the court opinion of his day, he felt obliged to resign.

The Adventures of Monsieur Guillaume

Regular dismissals from office (the penalty paid for his independence of mind) provided Malesherbes with time to indulge in his real vocation: botany.

In the seclusion of his château, he laid out the most extensive scientific garden in France and produced forty volumes of his *Herbier* (botanical notebooks).

In 1771, Malesherbes found the body of his wife in the woods near his house. She had killed herself with a musket.

In line with the political principles of the Enlightenment, Malesherbes believed that every man, even the king, should be subject to, **and have the benefit of**, the law.

As a consequence, Malesherbes too ended his life on the guillotine.

Denis Diderot

Diderot's bohemian tendencies often incurred the displeasure of his father, but his image of himself as an intellectual and a writer was definitively shaped by respect for the values of his father, the master craftsman. Diderot understood writing as a craft, requiring hard work and discipline.

Diderot always remained on excellent terms with his spinster sister, Denise, who developed a facial disfigurement and was obliged to wear artificial noses for the rest of her life. Another sister, Angélique, of her own accord, became an Ursuline nun. Later she went mad and died at the age of 28. Diderot's brother, Didier, became first an *abbé* and then a canon.

What these Christians call evangelical perfection is nothing but the deadly art of stifling nature. Didier would have been a good friend, a good brother, if Christ had not ordered him to trample all these trifles underfoot.

The "Secret History" of His Soul

In 1742, Diderot married the poor but beautiful Antoinette Champion, secretly and against his father's wishes. Only one of their children, Angélique, reached adulthood. Mme Diderot was seen by his friends as a difficult woman, but in his way, Diderot remained loyal.

In 1755, he met the great love of his life, Sophie Volland.

He appreciated her blunt and forthright way of expressing herself. The relationship lasted for a quarter of a century – until her death at the age of 68 finally separated them.

"The soul is a dark cavern, inhabited by all sorts of beneficent and maleficent beasts. The wicked man opens the cavern door and lets out only the latter. The man of good will does the opposite." Diderot

Diderot and Friends

"I was born as communicative as it is possible to be." Diderot was enthusiastic to the point of forgetting himself, amazingly knowledgeable and willing to be interested in, and if possible have a theory about, absolutely anything. All witnesses agree – Diderot was an ardent, unquenchable talker, ceaselessly pacing the room and tearing off his wig when some topic fired him.

It is on behalf of myself and of my friends that I read, that I reflect, that I write, meditate, listen, look and feel. In their absence, my devotion refers everything to them. I dream unceasingly of their happiness . . . It is to them that I have consecrated the use of all my senses and of all my faculties; and that is perhaps why, in my imagination and talk, everything gets slightly improved and exaggerated. They sometimes reproach me for this, the ungrateful wretches!

What is an *Encyclopédie*?

In an excellent article entitled "Encyclopédie", Diderot informed subscribers that the word comes from the Greek, meaning the "interrelation of all knowledge", an almost talismanic catchphrase evoked in many of Diderot's writings. "In truth the aim of an encyclopedia is to collect all the knowledge scattered over the face of the earth, to present its general outlines and structures to the men with whom we live and to transmit this to those who will come after us, so that the work of past centuries may be useful to the following centuries."

It could only belong to a philosophical age to attempt an encyclopedia . . . All things must be examined, debated, investigated without exception and without regard for anyone's feelings . . . We must overturn the barriers that reason never erected, give back to the arts and sciences the liberty that is so precious to them.

*The previous century pushed the sciences and arts as far as they could go . . . It is the task of the present century to assemble these achievements in a single **corpus** and transmit it to posterity.*

Art of the Enlightenment

The moral tableaux of **William Hogarth** (1697–1764) compare with the novels of Richardson and Fielding for richness of information. Satire in the popular visual genre was a tradition continued by **Thomas Rowlandson** (1756–1827) and **James Gillray** (1757–1815). **Thomas Gainsborough** (1727–88) and **Joshua Reynolds** (1723–92) produced portraits for wealthy patrons whose practical interests were illustrated by the horse portraits of **George Stubbs** (1724–1806) and the scientific and industrial tableaux of **Joseph Wright of Derby** (1734–97).

The art of Italy reflected the past glories of the Renaissance and Baroque in topographical masterpieces by **Antonio Canaletto** (1697–1768) and **Giambattista Tiepolo** (1696–1770). Depictions of Gothic ruins and imaginary prisons by **Giovanni Battista Piranesi** (1720–78) revealed a dark side of the Enlightenment imagination.

The splendid excesses of the French aristocracy were celebrated by the Rococo painters **Antoine Watteau** (1684–1721) and **François Boucher** (1703–70). Diderot reported on new paintings exhibited in the Parisian *salons*. His art criticism mixed moral judgements (he thought Boucher immoral) with aesthetic ones. In the artists he admired, **Jean–Siméon Chardin** (1699–1779), **Jean-Baptiste Greuze** (1725–1805) and **Jean-Honoré Fragonard** (1732–1806), he looked for a new moral vision, recognizable people and events in parallel to his speculations about new forms of drama.

The term "aesthetics" was coined by the German writer **A.G. Baumgarten** (1714–62), a pupil of the philosopher **Christian Wolff** (1679–1754); Baumgarten's *Aesthetica* was published in 1750. Classical archaeology and art history were founded by **Johann Joachim Winckelmann** (1717–68) who, together with the German painter **Anton Raphael Mengs** (1728–79), launched the revolutionary style of Neo-classicism in Rome circa 1750.

The writings of the **Earl of Shaftesbury** (1671–1713), a pupil of John Locke, were influential in the debate on "taste", as was the treatise by **Edmund Burke** (1729–97), *A Philosophical Inquiry into the Origin of Our Ideas of the Sublime and the Beautiful* (1756). **Immanuel Kant** (1724–1804) incorporated Analytics of the Beautiful and the Sublime in his *Critique of Judgement* (1790).

Jean-Jacques Rousseau (1712–78)

Rousseau was born in Geneva, a tiny Calvinist city-state republic in Switzerland surrounded by large and mainly Catholic duchies, principalities and kingdoms. Rousseau's mother died soon after giving birth to him and he received no formal education. At the age of 15, he was taken into the home of a Catholic Swiss baroness, Madame de Warens, who hoped to convert him and complete his education.

For the *Encyclopédie*, Rousseau wrote an article on "Political Economy" and most of the articles on musical subjects. Rousseau was accepted into the polite intellectual circles of Paris, and by the *philosophes* as one of their kind.

Rousseau's Challenge

With his first important essay, the *Discourse on the Arts and Sciences* (1749), Rousseau challenged a basic Enlightenment tenet and outlined a theme which he continued to develop in all of his later works.

I ARGUED THAT APPARENT CULTURAL AND SOCIAL PROGRESS HAS LED ONLY TO OUR REAL MORAL DEGRADATION. ALL OUR ARTS AND SCIENCES HAVE BEEN FORMED OUT OF IDLENESS AND ARE FED BY LUXURY!

Rousseau's next important essay, *Discourse on the Origins of Inequality* (1755), also paints a picture of human history as manifesting a progressive corruption and decadence. But now it is not sophistication, luxury and learning which are responsible, but **inequality**. And he traces the roots of inequality to **private property** and the envy it engenders.

Discourse on the Origins of Inequality

"Thus natural inequality unfolds itself insensibly with that of **combination**, and the difference between men, developed by their different circumstances, becomes more sensible and permanent in its effects, and begins to have an influence, in the same proportion, over the lot of individuals.

"It now became the interest of men to appear what they really were not. To be and to seem became totally different things; and from this distinction sprang insolent pomp and cheating trickery, with all the numerous vices that go in their train. On the other hand, free and independent as men were before, they were now, in consequence of new wants, brought into subjection, as it were, to all nature, and particularly to one another; and each became in some degree a slave even in becoming the master of other men: if rich, they stood in need of the services of others; if poor, of assistance; and even a middle condition did not enable them to do without one another . . . In a word, there arose rivalry and competition on the one hand, and conflicting interests on the other, together with a secret desire on both of profiting at the expense of others. All these evils were the first effects of **property**, and the inseparable attendants of growing inequality.

"Before the invention of **signs** to represent riches, wealth could hardly consist in anything but lands and cattle, the only real possession men can have . . . The wealthy, on their part, had no sooner begun to taste the pleasure of command, than they disdained all others . . . They (the rich) knew that they were founded on precarious and false titles; so that, if others took from them by force what they themselves had gained by force, they would have no reason to complain."

Voltaire vs. Rousseau

Rousseau sent a copy of this essay to Voltaire, who acknowledged receipt in a letter.

History, according to Rousseau, showed that progress had increased men's corruption, but he agreed that a time had arrived when the cause of that corruption, namely culture, was itself "needed to prevent its becoming worse . . . It is a case of leaving the weapon in the wound for fear that the victim would die if it were pulled out."

Nature and Natural History

During the first half of the 18th century, thinkers everywhere were still trying to digest the implications of Newtonian calculations. Speculations about the nature of man culminated in the model of "man the machine", a rather mechanical beast. Diderot, who had a good understanding of medicine and was fascinated by all the new developments in the life sciences, was drawn to speculate on their implications for our understanding of humankind. He was fascinated by the notion that everything in the universe was connected, and this led him into a host of intriguing – and farsighted – speculations and hypotheses.

I ask the natural scientist whether the universe or the general collection of all thinking and feeling molecules forms a whole or not. If he replies that it does not form a whole, he will be undermining with a single word the existence of God by introducing disorder into the universe, and he will be destroying the basis of philosophy by breaking the chain that links all beings.

Diderot, *Thoughts on the Interpretation of Nature*

Nature as a System: Linnaeus

The Swedish doctor and naturalist **Carl Linnaeus** (1707–78) distinguished sharply between living and non-living beings and helped establish the "life sciences", such as botany and zoology, as a separate area of investigation.

I ESTABLISHED A SYSTEM OF CLASSIFICATION FOR LIVING BEINGS BASED ON THEIR REPRODUCTIVE CHARACTERISTICS.

The binary system by which all living things are classified and given scientific names (identifying *genus*, or family name, and *species*, or individual name) is one we owe to Linnaeus. He saw nature as constituting a harmonious whole, an interrelated and balanced system created by God. His students roamed the world on commercial ships or with explorers such as Captain Cook.

Nature as History: Buffon

Linnaeus' views were challenged by **Georges-Louis Leclerc, Comte de Buffon** (1707–88). Beginning in 1749, he published 36 volumes of his *Histoire Naturelle* (*Natural History*) during his lifetime, supplemented by 8 volumes published (1788–1804) after his death. The work covered every subject in nature from man and birds to crustaceans, fishes and minerals, and was written in the most precise, elegant prose.

LINNAEUS' TAXONOMY IS JUST A LEARNED TECHNIQUE FOR MAKING THE WORLD SEEM **SIMPLER** THAN IT IS. I PROVIDE NOT A SYSTEM BUT A **DESCRIPTION** – OF A SERIES OF PARTICULAR AND CONTINGENT DETAILS.

He used fossil evidence and physical experimentation to argue that the world and life itself were far older than the theologians would admit. His title – natural *history* – drew attention to his belief that the world in its present state was not the state in which God had created it. His work was condemned by the theology faculty at the Sorbonne.

The Scandal of Materialism

Some of the *philosophes* most closely associated with the *Encyclopédie* developed a view of the world which was materialist, deterministic and atheistic.

All knowledge could be traced back to the sensations or impressions received from the outside world. Individual development was simply the cumulative result of such impressions. Traditional theological notions such as the "soul" seemed to be an "unnecessary hypothesis".

La Mettrie and Helvétius

The most scandalous and extreme materialist of the Enlightenment was a physician, **Julien Offroy de la Mettrie** (1709–51), whose *Homme Machine* (1747) claimed it was possible to explain all human faculties, intellectual and spiritual as well as physical, by the organization of matter, and thus to dispense with the need for any type of soul.

What was most scandalous to his contemporaries – including Diderot and d'Holbach – was la Mettrie's conclusion that there are **no absolute moral standards** and the individual is totally dominated by physical impulses. He was forced to flee, first Paris, then Holland. At the invitation of Frederick the Great, he settled finally in Prussia.

In July 1758, a friend of Diderot's, the freethinking philosopher **Claude-Adrien Helvétius** (1715–71), published a treatise *De l'Esprit* (*On Mind*), which provoked a violent scandal. Helvétius' materialism was of a behaviouristic type, extending the ideas of Locke and Condillac, explaining all human knowledge and conduct as the fruits of education through sensory and social experience. Helvétius refused to speculate about physiological factors, but nevertheless presented the challenge of deterministic understanding to any ethics.

Materialism and the Improvement of Human Beings

Helvétius believed that all men are born fundamentally equal in their faculties. Actual differences between men are due either to differences in the strength of their passions, or to accidents of their education.

De l'Esprit culminates in a vision of the improvement of human beings by the state. A wise legislator, by manipulating rewards for civic virtue, can affect the passions and thus overcome the inertia of the mind. This vision found an echo in the rhetoric of the French Revolution.

Holbach

Baron d'Holbach (1723–89), a German scientist, settled in Paris where he wrote over 400 articles, mainly on chemistry and mineralogy, for the *Encyclopédie*. Holbach was a generous host and his dinner parties were symposia for the leading Parisian radicals. Overseas visitors to his table included Laurence Sterne, Horace Walpole and Adam Smith from Britain; Cesare Bonesana, marchese di Beccaria, the great legal reformer from Milan, and Benjamin Franklin from America. While he was attached to the British Embassy in Paris, empiricist philosopher David Hume often dined at Holbach's.

The Factory of Freethinkers

After a journey to England in 1756 (where he spent some days with the actor David Garrick and also with a friend from his student days, the radical and libertine, John Wilkes), Baron d'Holbach decided that the time had come for a bolder campaign against received theological ideas.

I EMPLOYED A NUMBER OF YOUNG HELPERS AND SET UP A "FACTORY" WHICH TRANSLATED AND PROMOTED A TORRENT OF FREETHINKING WORKS.

Antiquity Unveiled, Priests Unmasked, Sacred Contagion (or *the Natural History of Superstition*), *Religious Cruelty, Essays on Prejudices, Hell Destroyed, A Critical History of Jesus Christ.*

Holbach's own *System of Nature* (1770) became an infamous "materialist" text. In it he proposed a thoroughgoing reductionist view. Man is a purely physical being. Physical man is Man acting under the impulsion of causes revealed to us by our senses. Moral man is Man acting through physical causes not directly revealed to us.

D'Alembert's Dream

Holbach's view of the human species is akin to that explored in nuanced and intriguing form by his friend Diderot in the *Rêve de d'Alembert* (*D'Alembert's Dream*, 1769), but which he never published. As a struggling young writer, Diderot had spent three years of his life translating from English an important medical dictionary. His fascination with the whole area was sustained throughout the decades of work on the *Encyclopédie*.

By outlining ideas in the form of a dialogue and a dream, Diderot emphasized their hypothetical character whose proof relied on future scientific discoveries.

The Dream

Two friends, Mlle de l'Espinasse and Bordeu, attend d'Alembert in his delirium.

The French *Parlements*

France in the 18th century was deeply divided over the questions of political authority. The king and his ministers were frequently in some sort of dispute with the *parlements*, the great French law courts dominated by the aristocracy, who claimed that these courts had the right to examine laws and reject those they did not like.

A ***PARLEMENT*** IS THE HIGHEST JUDICIAL BODY IN THE LAND.

IT ALSO FUNCTIONS AS A CENSOR OF THEATRE AND OF PUBLIC MORALS GENERALLY.

There were in all thirteen *parlements* in France, that of Paris exercising the most influence.

Offices in the *parlements* could be bought, and were hereditary; the higher ones bestowed nobility on their possessors who jealously insisted on the dignity of the "nobility of the robe" (*noblesse de la robe*) as against the "nobility of the sword" (*noblesse d'epée*).

Parlementariens were protocol-mad, and their processional return every November after their summer recess was one of the great ritual spectacles of the year.

THE KING'S EDICTS, TO BE ENFORCEABLE, HAVE TO BE "REGISTERED" BY **PARLEMENT.**

AND THIS GIVES US THE RIGHT TO CRITICIZE ROYAL POLICY BY WAY OF A "REMONSTRANCE".

As a result, *parlement* was, for good or bad, the centre of legalized opposition to absolute monarchy, and through all the middle years of the century it was in continual conflict with the throne. The Palais de Justice, home of the Paris *parlement*, was, in the words of Simon Schama, "virtually a miniature city in itself".

Montesquieu's Spirit of the Laws

Montesquieu's *Esprit des Lois* (*The Spirit of the Laws*), first published in 1748, lent political respectability and wide currency to the view that the *parlements* needed to limit the prerogatives of the crown. Montesquieu was himself a president of the *parlement* of Bordeaux.

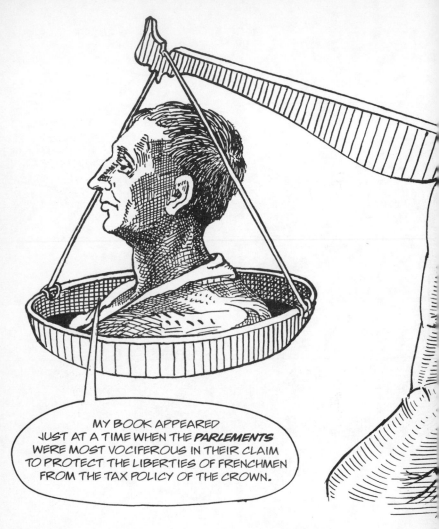

MY BOOK APPEARED JUST AT A TIME WHEN THE *PARLEMENTS* WERE MOST VOCIFEROUS IN THEIR CLAIM TO PROTECT THE LIBERTIES OF FRENCHMEN FROM THE TAX POLICY OF THE CROWN.

It became an overnight best-seller, going through twelve editions in six months. In 1762, the ultimate accolade was bestowed on the work when Alexandre Deleyre produced a handbook of edited extracts, the *Génie de Montesquieu*, designed for polemical use.

Montesquieu was looking for the reasons which would explain why political institutions were the way they were. He set out to survey the great variety of social and political orders with two principles: the *uniformity* of human nature and the *diversity* produced by environment and culture. Montesquieu's study is the first great classic of what we can recognize as sociological literature, and it transformed the nature of philosophical debate about politics.

THERE ARE CERTAIN LAWS OF NATURE THAT APPLY TO ALL MEN, SINCE THEY ARE DERIVED FROM THE CONSTITUTION OF OUR BEING.

Natural Law

Like many of his contemporaries, Montesquieu looked back to an ancient tradition of **Natural Law** theory. Stoics such as **Cicero** (106–43 BC) thought it the ethical duty of man to think beyond custom and practice in order to discover what it was he *ought* to do.

Enlightenment writers would sometimes speak of God as the author of the natural law and as the source of its authority, "but in actuality they all derived its origin and binding quality from the nature of man, the agreement of wise men across the world and through history, the testimony of reason, man's natural sense of justice, and, as Diderot put it in a revolutionary if still tentative way in the *Encyclopédie*, the infallible general will of men." [Peter Gay]

An Unkempt Masterpiece

The first third of *The Spirit of the Laws* deals with the nature and forms of government and the rights of subjects. Then the book turns to an analysis of the influence of climate and environment on politics and social customs. The last part of the book is a rag-bag containing discussions, among other things, of political economy, politics in France and legal theory.
The Spirit of the Laws is the most unkempt masterpiece of the 18th century.

YOUR BOOK IS A LABYRINTH WITHOUT A CLUE, LACKING ALL METHOD.

I POSTULATE A "SPIRIT" BEHIND EACH FORM OF GOVERNMENT.

Behind monarchies was "honour" – that ingrained sense of status and responsibility demonstrated by a working nobility. The spirit behind republics was "virtue", a sense of civic consciousness, of belonging and the duties which that entails. The spirit behind despotism was "fear". When any of these supporting spirits weakened, the government itself would weaken.

Individual Liberty and The Rule of Law

All of the *philosophes* could agree on the noble and humane philosophy embodied in *The Spirit of the Laws*. Montesquieu's passionate belief in individual liberty is clearest in his treatment of issues relating to law and justice.

I believe that despotism is always bad and needs to be checked. I particularly approve of what I see as a sense of liberty enjoyed by British subjects, which I attribute to the separation of powers within the British political system.

In Montesquieu's account, the king was the only executive power, while Parliament alone could make the laws; and a judiciary functioned independently of them both.

In fact, Montesquieu's was a highly simplified view of British politics. And he was writing at a time of change in Britain. England's leading thinkers tended to conservatism. There was no need for radical ideologues after John Locke's definition of political liberalism and a modern economic liberalism were in place. Indeed, England's earlier radicalism was turned against it by the American colonists. Montesquieu's book certainly influenced them and the political theorists of the Scottish Enlightenment.

Enlightening the Despots

The political writings of the Enlightenment are in the main directed against what was often loosely termed "despotism", which covered a multitude of sins. It included any arbitrary exercise of power by the monarch, but also referred to privileges claimed by the aristocracy and the Church, in so far as these claims were made simply on the basis of tradition, precedent or authority.

Against such irrational residues or survivals, the Enlightenment upholds an ideal of bringing every member of the nation, even the king, within the scope of the law . . .

Montesquieu's arguments for a form of limited monarchy persuaded many thinkers in the mid-18th century, among them the Physiocrats, advocates of free trade and commercial liberalism under the Ancien Régime, who remained monarchists.

Later, as democratic and republican sentiments were stirred among a new generation of agitators, these were able to borrow a visionary language from Rousseau's writings. But most of the key figures of the High Enlightenment were **reformers** and not radicals at all. It seemed natural to them to address their arguments to those who actually wielded power.

Several of the *philosophes* – including Voltaire, Diderot and Helvétius – were for a time captivated by the idea of "enlightened despotism". Or perhaps we should say, of "*enlightening* despotism", because enlightened despotism was not a political theory, not even for the *philosophes*. But it was an important career opportunity. Politically marginal in France, they turned to reforming monarchs, like Frederick in Prussia and Catherine in Russia, who were inclined to religious toleration and appeared committed to the rational reform of political, legal and economic life.

Frederick II of Prussia

Frederick II ("the Great") of Prussia (1712–86) engaged the imagination of many of the *philosophes*. In 1736, while still crown prince, he had written an attack on what was generally seen as the cynicism of Machiavelli's political philosophy, and he proved his interest in art, music and poetry. And Frederick had begun a correspondence with Voltaire. As Voltaire was keen for all his friends to know, it was Frederick who had taken the initiative.

In the summer of 1750, Voltaire turned his back on Paris (which he would not revisit until his triumphant return in the last year of his life) and began a three-year sojourn at the court of Frederick the Great. He became disillusioned when he discovered that his political and philosophical ideas were not much valued by Frederick. In fact, no service was required of him other than to amuse Frederick and to correct, and praise, his French verses.

Catherine the Great of Russia

Catherine II (1729–96), who succeeded to the Russian throne in 1762, had wider views. She showed a determination to make much-needed changes in Russia's social and political structures. She had been influenced by Montesquieu and by the Italian legal theorist, **Cesare Beccaria** (1738–94), and was deeply impressed by the achievements of the *Encyclopédistes*.

In the mid-1760s, Diderot was nearing the end of his work on the *Encyclopédie*. He had received few honours and distinctions and had experienced a period of profound doubt and gloom.

For some years afterwards, Diderot acted as Catherine's unofficial "cultural attaché". In 1773, Catherine lured Diderot to make the long journey to St. Petersburg, his only significant journey outside of France.

Diderot pictured his position in Russia as that of one who had been sent for, across Europe, to instruct a monarch – to act the part of Socrates to Catherine's Alcibiades. It was a dream-like fulfilment of his fantasies; for he believed, as did other "enlightened" thinkers, that social progress had to be handed down from above and that reformers had to secure the ears of the great. "To whom should a philosopher address himself forcefully," he had written in *Pages Against a Tyrant* (1769), "if not a sovereign?"

It was rumoured that the empress had to place a table between herself and Diderot to protect herself from his energetic gestures.

Instructions to the Empress

Diderot sought to rekindle the liberal ambitions which had been held by this formidable woman. But she was quite shrewd and confident enough to feel untouched by his admonitions. Afterwards, Diderot wrote up the details of their conversations together.

It seems to me that the source of all political and civil power can only be the consent of the nation . . .

There is no true sovereign but the nation; there can be no true legislator but the people . . . Laws are useless if there is a single member of society who may infringe them with impunity.

The first line of a well-conceived code of law ought to bind the sovereign.

The Priest and the Philosopher

The priest, whose philosophic system is a tissue of absurdities, secretly tends to maintain ignorance; reason is the enemy of faith, and faith is the foundation of the priest's position, his fortune, and his prestige . . .

The philosopher speaks very ill of the priest; the priest speaks very ill of the philosopher. But the philosopher has never killed any priests, whereas the priest has killed a great many philosophers. Nor has the philosopher ever killed any kings, whereas the priest has killed a great many . . . Diderot

Philosophers Will Never Form a Religious Sect

"We should not fear that any philosophical opinion will ever harm the religion of a country. Though our demonstrations clash directly with our mysteries, that is nothing to the purpose, for the latter are not less revered upon that account by our Christian philosophers, who know very well that the objects of reason and those of faith are of a very different nature.

"*Philosophers will never form a religious sect,* the reason of which is, their writings are not calculated for the common people, and they themselves are free from enthusiasm.

"If we divide mankind into twenty parts, it will be found that nineteen of these consist of persons employed in manual labour, who will never know that such a man as Mr Locke existed. In the remaining twentieth part, how few are readers? And among such as are so, twenty amuse themselves with romances to one who studies philosophy. The thinking part of mankind is confined to a very small number, and these will never disturb the peace and tranquillity of the world.

"Neither Montaigne, Locke, Bayle, Spinoza, Hobbes, Lord Shaftesbury, Collins, nor Toland, lighted up the firebrand of discord in their countries; this has generally been the work of divines, being at first desirous of being the head of a party. But what do I say? *All the works of modern philosophers put together will never raise so much commotion as did the dispute among the Franciscans, over the cut of their sleeves and cowls.*"

From "On Mr Locke" by Voltaire, in *Philosophical Letters from England* (1733)

To Voltaire, Frederick the Great wrote: "The fabric of superstition is tottering on its foundation and is about to collapse. The nations will write in their histories that Voltaire was the promoter of the revolution that took place in men's minds during the eighteenth century . . ."

The Catholic Church in France

In France, the Catholic Church was affected by a deep malaise. Parish priests lived in grinding poverty, doing their work with little help from their superiors. The bishops, usually from noble families, lived in sumptuous palaces. Many neglected their duties and felt free to hold unorthodox beliefs.

The behaviour of the clergy was probably not much worse in the 18th century than it had been in preceding centuries. But the tales told in taverns ever since the Middle Ages had left a rich fund of stock characters.

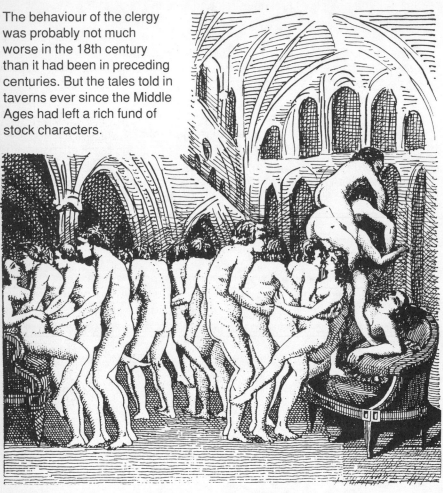

Lascivious monks, ruttish nuns, impotent bishops succumbing to venereal disease, and lesbian abbesses surrendering to "uterine fury" . . .

The clergy were an easy target for slander, and make frequent appearances in the pornography which proliferated in the world of the Enlightenment.

The Age of Enlightenment as an Age of Faith

The repeated attacks on the power of the Catholic Church by the leading *philosophes* can give rise to the impression that it was in a particularly strong position and militant mood during the period of the Enlightenment. In fact, in the various nations of Europe, the 18th century saw the institutions of the state gaining in power and influence at the expense of the established churches, Catholic or Protestant.

It would be wrong to portray the 18th century as one in which faith was constantly on the defence against the onward march of reason. The Age of Enlightenment also saw the development of powerful religious movements.

- In England, the beginnings of Methodism
- In the North American colonies, the "Great Awakening"
- The rise of the mystical Hassidic sect within the Polish Jewry
- In the German Protestant states, the Pietist movement

The Social Necessity of Religion

An anecdote, probably apocryphal, was widely circulated, in which Voltaire was represented as entertaining fellow *philosophes* at his home at Ferney. The company is talking animatedly and frankly about atheism. Suddenly Voltaire silences everyone and sends the servants out of the room. He then justifies his precaution by asking, "Do you want your throats cut tonight?"

Putting the Fear of Hell . . .

Although Voltaire and many other *philosophes* doubted the truths adhered to by the theologians, they nevertheless felt that religion was probably socially necessary. The fear of hell and eternal damnation could still function as an effective instrument of social control – as **Edward Gibbon** (1737–94) noted in *The Decline and Fall of the Roman Empire* (1776).

The various modes of worship which prevailed in the Roman world were all considered by the people as equally true, by the philosopher as equally false, and by the magistrates as equally useful.

The Church, the State and Civil Rights

Religious toleration was difficult for many rulers to implement formally. The great majority of states were governed by monarchies whose legitimacy stemmed at least in part from their allegiance to a particular church. The French monarch, whose subjects included a sizeable number of Protestants, took a coronation oath to extirpate Protestant heresy. The English monarch was secular head of the Church of England. The King of Prussia was *summus episcopus* of the Lutheran church.

Maria Theresa of Austria (1717–80)

Joseph II (1741–90)

In 1782, Emperor Joseph II issued a Patent of Toleration which granted the Jews of Austria a number of important civil liberties.

Frederick II of Prussia came to the throne in 1740, the same year as Maria Theresa. Although officially the head of the majority Lutheran church, Frederick was personally an unbeliever and a Freemason. He defined his role as that of holding the ring between the many different religious groups in Prussia, even to the extent of allotting state funds for the building of a new Catholic cathedral in his capital Berlin in 1747. Heresy inquiries and public exposition of theological controversy were forbidden. In 1750, the Jews in Prussia were granted increased rights.

Moses Mendelssohn (1728–86), Jewish thinker and writer who rose from the poverty of the Dessau ghetto, was a brilliant figure of the German Enlightenment. He was a revolution all by himself, who influenced Christian society in Berlin to review its attitude to Jews. Mendelssohn provided his friend, the dramatist **Gotthold Lessing** (1729–81), with the model for his play *Nathan the Wise*.

Freemasonry

In 1717, London saw the establishment of the first Freemasons' Lodge in England. The Freemasons achieved remarkable importance during the 18th century. Part of their success was due to the involvement of aristocrats and even reigning princes such as Frederick the Great of Prussia and Francis I of Austria. For a while, Benjamin Franklin and Voltaire were members of the same Masonic lodge.

MEMBERS VOWED TO CAST ASIDE DISTINCTIONS OF RANK IN PURSUIT OF CERTAIN KEY IDEALS OF THE ENLIGHTENMENT.

WE AIMED AT MORAL REGENERATION WITHOUT REFERENCE TO THE ESTABLISHED CHURCHES.

IN MY OPERA, *THE MAGIC FLUTE* (1791), I MADE USE OF MY EXPERIENCE AS A FREEMASON TO CREATE A VISION OF REASON, BEAUTY AND LOVE.

Mozart

Freemasonry was a mixture of weird mystic rituals with secular, utopian and universalist ideals such as fraternity, equality, religious toleration and reason. Freemasons were condemned by Pope Benedict XIV in 1751, and they were politically suspect in the German states.

When the Founding Fathers of the American Revolution, most of whom were Freemasons, came to draft the Constitution of the United States, they made no mention of God. **Thomas Jefferson** (1743–1826) and **James Madison** (1751–1836) specifically sought to exclude religion from public life and politics.

119

The Great Watchmaker

The Enlightenment came more and more to identify God with the laws of Nature. It was the regularity of Nature, unveiled by the Newtonian sciences, that provided the most reliable and accessible manifestation of the divinity. The whole universe with its beauty, vastness and intricate design, testified to His presence and His superb skill. Like a Great Watchmaker, He had created the world and given it immutable laws to run by, and then had withdrawn.

The Scepticism of David Hume

The trouble was that traditional Christianity looked for proof of the divinity of Christ in the miracles attested to in the Gospels. Miracles, such as the raising of Lazarus from the dead, or the very Resurrection itself, all involved an overthrow of those very laws of nature which many in the Enlightenment were so eager to identify with God. **David Hume** (1711–76), a chief figure of the Scottish Enlightenment, went further than most.

A MIRACLE IS A VIOLATION OF THE LAWS OF NATURE; THE PROOF AGAINST A MIRACLE, FROM THE VERY NATURE OF THE FACT, IS AS ENTIRE AS ANY ARGUMENT FROM EXPERIENCE CAN POSSIBLY BE IMAGINED.

OUR EVIDENCE FOR THE TRUTH OF THE CHRISTIAN RELIGION IS LESS THAN OUR EVIDENCE FOR THE TRUTH OF OUR SENSES.

David Hume was the author of the most formidable attacks on the rationality of belief in God ever mounted by a philosopher. Many philosophers before Hume had been accused of being atheists. Hume was the first great philosopher who admitted it. His friends persuaded him not to publish his finest work, *Dialogues Concerning Natural Religion* (1779), during his lifetime.

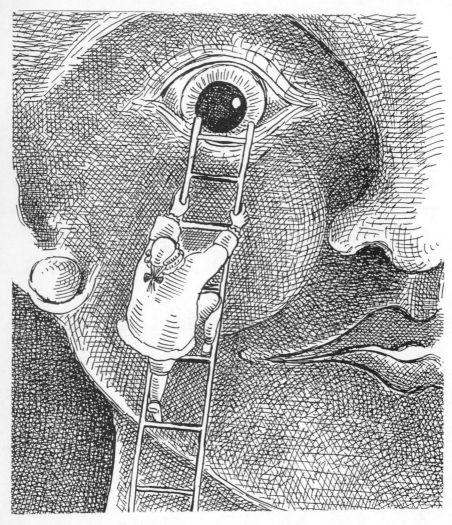

*I have no argument with the idea of a Creator, but any statement claiming to describe His qualities or characteristics must be utterly illogical. Belief cannot be in any way **rationally** defended.*

A Treatise of Hum(e)an Nature

Hume's *A Treatise of Human Nature* (1739–40) was completed when he was just 26 years of age. Its subtitle admitted to *Being an Attempt to Introduce the Experimental Method of Reasoning into Moral Subjects*. It extends and applies the empirical psychology pioneered by John Locke.

Men are now cured of their passion for hypotheses and systems in natural philosophy, and will harken to no arguments but those which are derived from observation. It is full time that they should attempt a like reformation in all moral disputations; and reject every system of ethics, however subtle or ingenious, which is not founded on fact and observations.

Hume's scepticism was so radical that it threatened to undermine the very concept on which science itself rested: **causality**. Using the example of a billiard ball cannoning around the billiard table, he points out that we can distinguish a cause from an effect, but that we cannot experience "causality".

We see the motion of the first billiard ball (the cause, if you will) as it careers towards the second. We see the motion (or effect) of the second ball, after it has been struck. But we cannot isolate or experience causality itself.

Science appears to be resting on a foundation as shaky as that of religion.

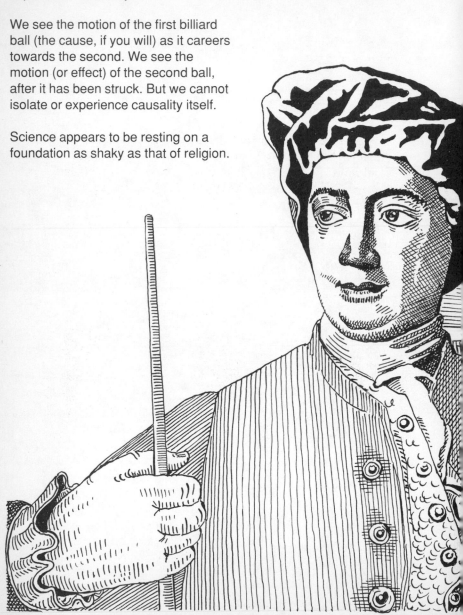

Hume's scepticism not only threatened the unity of the external world, but even the world of experience itself. In Hume's anguished meditations, the "self" fragments. It presents itself as a mere bundle of perceptions. Each particular experience is tied to a particular moment in time. A moment later a different impression is created. Nothing ties the two sensations together except custom or habit. The "self" is fiction.

Where am I, or what? From what causes do I derive my existence, and to what condition shall I return? . . . I am confounded with all these questions and begin to fancy myself in the most deplorable condition imaginable, inviron'd with the deepest darkness, and utterly depriv'd of every member and faculty.

The philosopher **Bertrand Russell** (1872–1970) comments that in the latter portions of the *Treatise*, Hume forgets all about his fundamental doubts, and writes much as any other enlightened moralist of his time might have written; he applies to his doubts the remedy that he recommends, namely "carelessness and inattention".

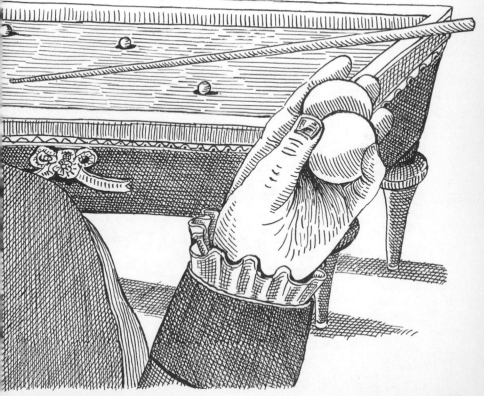

Music of the Enlightenment

As public concerts increased and opera houses flourished, these provided some alternative to the traditional patronage of the Church and court. Italian musicians such as **Antonio Vivaldi** (1678–1741) and **Domenico Scarlatti** (1685–1757) gave an early lead. Vivaldi's huge output of sacred music and operas also included over 450 concertos. Scarlatti, who wrote over 500 sonatas for the keyboard, was the son of **Alessandro Scarlatti** (1660–1725), founder of the Neapolitan school of opera. In 1735, **Giovanni Battista Pergolesi** (1710–36), knowing he was soon to die, retired to a monastery to write his *Stabat Mater*, a sensuous piece of religious music which made him famous. In 1752 a performance of Pergolesi's comic opera, *La serva padrona*, sparked off a battle in Paris, "The War of Buffoons", over the respective merits of the new Italian opera and the classical French style in the tradition of **Jean-Baptiste Lully** (1632–87), whose foremost representative was **Jean-Philippe Rameau** (1683–1764). The *Encyclopédistes* were deeply implicated in this tumult. Rousseau, who wrote most of the musical articles for the *Encyclopédie*, was also the composer of a successful Italian-style opera, *Le Devin du village*. Rousseau's advocacy of naturalism in opera – with music serving the dramatic action – was developed by **Christoph Gluck** (1714–87) who worked in Paris and Vienna.

Large-scale works were often religious in nature, like the *St Matthew Passion* (1729) of **J.S. Bach** (1685–1750); but Bach also wrote secular music, such as the *Brandenburg Concertos* (1721). His sons, **C.P.E.** and **J.C. Bach**, became important composers of the 18th century.

Vivaldi   D. Scarlatti   A. Scarlatti   Pergolesi

Georg Friedrich Handel (1685–1759) came to England in 1710. In 1732, Covent Garden Opera House was founded in London, and Handel established himself as a composer of 50 Italian-style operas. He also wrote 20 oratorios, of which his *Messiah* (first performed in Dublin in 1742) is the best-known, and music for royal celebrations. **John Gay** (1685–1732) satirized the fashion for Italianate opera in his play, *The Beggar's Opera* (1728), which incorporated popular street ballads of the day.

For almost 30 years, **Franz Josef Haydn** (1732–1809) was employed by Prince Esterhazy, years in which he wrote 104 symphonies, 80 string quartets, 52 piano sonatas, operas and choral music. Several *philosophes* heard the seven-year-old prodigy **Wolfgang Amadeus Mozart** (1756–91) play in Paris. Mozart died in poverty, but his last years produced magnificent symphonies and great operas – *The Marriage of Figaro* (1786), *Don Giovanni* (1787), *Cosi fan tutte* (1790) and *The Magic Flute* (1791) – which typify the Enlightenment.

Savage Rousseau

Rousseau was turning himself into a bitter enemy of "sophistication" in all its forms. Not only was his animosity towards the rich clear (and it frightened Voltaire), but it extended towards many of his fellow *philosophes* as they paraded their intellectual wares.

WHAT ARE WE TO THINK OF THESE COMPILERS WHO HAVE RASHLY BROKEN OPEN THE DOOR OF THE SCIENCES AND INTRODUCED INTO THEIR SANCTUARY A POPULACE UNWORTHY TO APPROACH IT?

By the mid-1750s, Rousseau was growing more and more out of sympathy with the Holbach circle and Paris generally. There were several heated quarrels with other *Encyclopédistes*. He was sick of the "*salons* and fountains and tiresome people who wanted to show them off", sick of the "pamphlets and clavichords and card-games and stupid *bon-mots,* the little tellers of tales and the givers of great suppers." (1756)

Voyage to the Interior

"I have met many men who were more learned than I in their philosophizing, but their philosophy remained as it were external to them. Wishing to know more than other people, they studied the workings of the universe, as they might have studied some machine they had come across, out of sheer curiosity. They studied human nature in order to speak knowledgeably about it, not in order to know themselves; their efforts were directed to the instruction of others and not to their own inner enlightenment."

Rousseau's Confessions

Rousseau presented a dazzling one-man alternative Enlightenment that reached an exceptionally wide audience because he packaged his ideas in a best-selling novel, *La Nouvelle Héloïse* (1761), then in an educational treatise that read like a novel, *Emile* (1762). The reading public were eager for another story – that of his life.

In January 1762, Rousseau settled down to give an account of himself to Malesherbes in a series of letters which later formed the nucleus of his *Confessions* (1781–88).

I DO NOT FEAR TO BE SEEN AS I AM. I KNOW MY FAULTS AND I AM VERY CONSCIOUS OF MY VICES, BUT I DIE FULL OF HOPE IN THE SUPREME GOD AND WHOLLY PERSUADED THAT OF ALL THE MEN I HAVE KNOWN IN MY LIFE, NONE WAS BETTER THAN I.

The *philosophes* were an urbane, secular and gregarious bunch. Rousseau always burnt with a religious fire. The *philosophes* looked to one another in striving to define and defend a new code of virtue that was modern and public. Rousseau set up his **own** conscience as the only touchstone on issues of morality.

Diderot warned his friend of the dangers of this kind of subjectivism.

Rousseau's fierce concern for his own inner being was a sign of a predisposition towards paranoia. But even someone paranoid can be persecuted. Rousseau suffered real persecution and his paranoia worsened. At one point, his house was stoned. He took refuge on the Ile de Saint Pierre, but was expelled by the Bernese authorities.

Later in Paris, the good-natured David Hume offered to help him find asylum in England. On the evening before their departure in 1766, Baron d'Holbach gave Hume a warning.

Thérèse, Rousseau's wife, did not join him in London until later. Hume, on learning that her escort was the notorious libertine James Boswell (the biographer of Dr Johnson), dreaded an event "fatal to our friend's honour". We have it from the stallion's mouth that Hume's fears were fully justified.

The First Romantic

As Rousseau explained to Malesherbes: "I would seek out some wild spot in the forest." In a vast solitary space, his spirit lost itself. "I do not think, I do not reason. I feel myself, with a kind of voluptuousness, possessed of the substance of the universe . . . a sweet and profound reverie takes hold of the senses so that you lose yourself, with a delicious intoxication, in the immensity of that splendid system with which you identify yourself; and then all particular things escape you, and you only see and feel the whole."

Adam Smith (1723–90)

Adam Smith, like his friend David Hume, was a key figure of the Scottish Enlightenment. He was the only child of a family in comfortable circumstances in Kirkcaldy, a village on the shores of the Firth of Forth. His father, a customs official, died a few months before his birth, and Adam remained close to his mother all his life. Before his fourth birthday he was stolen by a band of gypsies, and it was some time before he could be found.

Smith entered Balliol College, Oxford, as a scholarship student in 1740 but described the university as "steeped in port and prejudice".

IN THE UNIVERSITY OF OXFORD, THE GREATER PART OF THE PUBLIC PROFESSORS HAVE, FOR THESE MANY YEARS, GIVEN UP ALTOGETHER EVEN THE PRETENCE OF TEACHING.

University authorities confiscated Adam Smith's copy of David Hume's recently published *Treatise of Human Nature* (1739), which had been presented to him by his teacher in Glasgow, the philosopher **Francis Hutcheson** (1694–1746).

Back in Scotland, Smith gave a series of public lectures on English literature, a completely new subject, to an audience of 100 citizens who paid a guinea each. Then in 1750–51 he offered a public course on economics, a subject never yet heard of in Oxford's sanctimonious halls. This earned Smith a chair at the University of Glasgow, first as professor of logic, then as professor of moral philosophy.

Andrew Cochrane, the Provost of the city of Glasgow, had just founded a Political Economy Club and enrolled Smith as a member.

A Theory of Moral Sentiments

Smith's first work, his *Theory of Moral Sentiments* (1759) is a judicious survey of philosophical ethics, its nature and its psychology. It showed Smith's knack for simple explanations of complex problems. He described the moral sentiment by a simple figure of speech, an "inner man", an **impartial spectator** within each of us who passes judgement on everything we do from the point of view of other people.

I CONSIDER WHAT I SHOULD SUFFER IF I WERE REALLY YOU.

David Hume wrote from London to report on the success of his friend's book.

The public seem to applaud it extremely. It was looked for by the foolish people with some impatience; and the mob of literati are beginning already to be loud in its praises.

Smith resigned his chair at Glasgow University in order to work as tutor to the young Duke of Buccleuch, and especially to accompany the Duke on the European Grand Tour. As well as meeting Voltaire in Geneva and his friend David Hume in Paris, Smith was enlisted in the French equivalent of the Political Economy Club by **François Quesnay** (1694–1774). Quesnay was the king's doctor, installed at Versailles by Madame de Pompadour.

Quesnay's disciples in economics later became famous as the Physiocrats, who held that production, not exchange, creates wealth and the surplus available for accumulation. Adam Smith felt completely at home and continued to work on his big book, the *Wealth of Nations*.

Wealth of Nations, 1776

Smith's *Wealth of Nations* opens with the famous example of a pin factory, based on the Glasgow ironworks called the nailery, which he had enjoyed visiting while still at school. The division of labour made it possible for ten people to turn out 48,000 pins in a single day.

Smith disapproved of any government interference in what he saw as the natural dynamics of supply and demand. Free trade is the cornerstone of his political economy. His work provided arguments for the elimination of tariffs, duties and monopolies, and the encouragement of free-market enterprise on the part of individuals. In these points, Smith was in agreement with the *laissez-faire* policies advocated by the Physiocrats.

The Invisible Hand

In Smith's account, market relations encourage the freedom of individuals as well as those of nations. It is by means of the key market transaction – the buying and selling of labour – that the labouring poor had become free to contract for their wages, to leave harsh conditions and seek better ones.

Even if the individual labourers – and indeed the working classes as a whole – suffer an increase in relative inequality, they nevertheless enjoy an absolute improvement in their standards of living. So, despite being based on individuals pursuing their own self-interest, the system reveals an "invisible hand" which advances the interests of society. Social inequality is reconciled with adequate provision for the poorest.

Smith and Rousseau

Smith recognizes that there is a darker side to the division of labour. Being confined to a few very simple operations, the labourer must eventually become "as stupid and ignorant as it is possible for a human creature to become". His account of dehumanization is as explicit and clear-eyed as any modern account of industrial alienation.

IN MODERN COMMERCIAL SOCIETY, MEN HAVE ENSLAVED THEMSELVES BY BECOMING ADDICTED TO LUXURY AND BY MULTIPLYING THE FALSE NEEDS WHICH THEY HAVE CREATED.

I DO NOT SHARE YOUR ANXIETY, MONSIEUR ROUSSEAU. I ASSUME THAT INDIVIDUAL LIBERTY IS INALIENABLE.

If they choose, men can keep their distance from the "great scramble of society" by learning to judge their own conduct from the vantage point of an impartial spectator, in the manner earlier outlined in the *Theory of Moral Sentiments*.

Smith and Rousseau both present a narrative of human history in which economics and morals are intertwined, a passage of humankind from savage simplicity to the modern world of private property, sophistication and inequality.

Smith conceives of an original "state of nature" as one of scarcity. Human freedom results only from the spiral of historical development by which cooperation in production and exchange leads to a division of labour and the creation of surplus.

Adam Smith on the market in ideas: "In opulent or commercial society, besides, to think or reason comes to be, like every other employment, a particular business, which is carried on by a very few people, who furnish the public with all the thought and reason possessed by the vast multitudes that labour. Only a very small part of any ordinary person's knowledge has been the product of personal observation or reflection. All the rest has been purchased, in the same manner as his shoes or his stockings, from those whose business it is to make up and prepare for the market that particular species of goods."

Samuel Johnson (1709–84)

Born the son of a Lichfield bookseller, Johnson was already well-read when he went to Oxford, but lack of money forced him to withdraw from his studies. He finally received his doctorate in 1764 and was pleased to become "Dr Johnson".

Johnson lived and worked in comparative obscurity, scratching a living as a journalist and translator in Birmingham, before settling in London in 1737 where he eventually became the dominant literary figure. From 1747 until 1755, he worked on his most ambitious project, *A Dictionary of the English Language,* for which he himself wrote all of the more than 40,000 entries. His lavish use of literary quotations was a real innovation. Johnson's *Dictionary* remained the most authoritative until the *Oxford English Dictionary* appeared in 1884.

In 1763, ambitious young Scotsman **James Boswell** (1740–95) travelled to London specifically in order to make the acquaintance of the great man.

I IMMORTALIZED HIM IN MY *LIFE OF SAMUEL JOHNSON* (1791), THE RESULT OF TWENTY YEARS OF CLOSE, THOUGH UNEQUAL, FRIENDSHIP.

In 1764, Johnson founded "The Club", where he enjoyed the companionship of men like the painter Sir Joshua Reynolds, the parliamentarian Edmund Burke and the playwright Oliver Goldsmith.

Smith Joins Dr Johnson's Literary Club

In the spring of 1773, Adam Smith went to London with what he thought was a nearly completed manuscript of the *Wealth of Nations*. There he dined with Dr Johnson, Edmund Burke, Edward Gibbon, David Garrick, Sir Joshua Reynolds and Oliver Goldsmith.

Benjamin Franklin (1706–90)

Benjamin Franklin was in his own way an Enlightenment archetype: a backwoodsman ("noble savage") and autodidact who became a leading scientist with an interest in everything. His experiments with lightning and electricity acquired emblematic importance for an age obsessed with the new powers of science and technology. For decades, Franklin published *Poor Richard's Almanack,* a cross between an encyclopedia, a journal and a collection of parables aimed at self-help and self-improvement.

Franklin was known in the Paris *salons* as a true *philosophe* and scientist, even before the American Revolution became a cause of such excitement and celebration in Europe.

The American Revolution

A boundless optimistic faith in progress and equal opportunity found its 18th century home in America, which appeared to embody the Enlightenment in action.

Declaration of the Rights of Man

The American colonials were reluctant rebels. For decades, they directed thoughtful petitions and arguments at the English government, asking only that they be allowed the same liberties enjoyed by English subjects at home.

Eventually they were driven to wage a War of Independence. The Declaration of Independence with its ringing, unforgettable formulations, begins with a paraphrase of the principles first asserted by John Locke at the time of England's own "Glorious Revolution".

"We hold these Truths to be self-evident, that all Men are created equal, that they are endowed by their Creator with certain unalienable Rights, that among these are Life, Liberty, and the Pursuit of Happiness."

John Locke had spoken only of Life, Liberty and *Property*. But in the "land of opportunity", even those with very little Property could pursue their own happiness. America's reluctant revolutionaries were fortunate. They were never confronted with the spectacle of hungry and underemployed masses. In the New World even the poor were able to turn to useful toil and so escape the wretchedness and obscurity to which so many in Europe were condemned.

When he observed the state of the poorest Parisians, Benjamin Franklin found himself thinking "often of the happiness of New England . . ."

In the Old World, of twenty millions of people, there are nineteen millions more wretched, more accursed in every circumstance of human existence than the most conspicuously wretched individual in the whole United States.

The Poor and the Slaves

The New World was not without its poor. In fact, the Founding Fathers were convinced that the distinction between rich and poor was an eternal one. They were allowed to pursue their revolution and hold on to that belief. Later, in the French Revolution, the demands of the most wretched part of society helped to precipitate the extremist violence of the Reign of Terror.

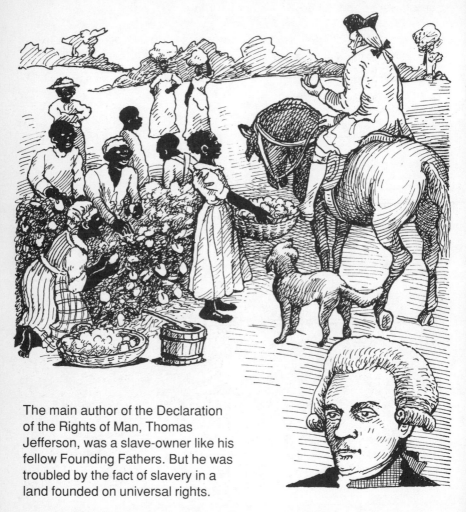

The main author of the Declaration of the Rights of Man, Thomas Jefferson, was a slave-owner like his fellow Founding Fathers. But he was troubled by the fact of slavery in a land founded on universal rights.

I tremble for my country when I reflect that God is just, that his justice cannot sleep forever. Commerce between master and slave is despotism. Nothing is more certainly written in the book of fate than that these people are to be free.

Condemnation of Slavery

Several representatives of the Enlightenment followed the example of Montesquieu and condemned slavery as a practice unworthy of civilized man and running counter to the enlightened belief in a common humanity.

But principled opposition to slavery came in the main from the evangelists among Quakers, Methodists and Anglicans who condemned slave ownership as sinful. In 1787 the Abolition Society was established in Britain, followed a year later by the Amis des Noirs in France.

The Defence of Slavery

And in all sectors of society, the defence of slavery was more common than is generally recognized. James Boswell, after reporting Samuel Johnson's opposition to slavery, begs leave to present his own "most solemn protest against his general doctrine with respect to the Slave Trade":

"To abolish a status, which in all ages God has sanctioned, and man has continued, would not only be robbery to an innumerable class of our fellow-subjects; but it would be extreme cruelty to the African Savages, a portion of whom it saves from massacre, or intolerable bondage in their own country, and introduces into a much happier state of life; especially now when their passage to the West-Indies and their treatment there is humanely regulated."

Immanuel Kant (1724–1804)

The German Enlightenment was a belated one, but it did produce a giant of philosophy: Immanuel Kant. He began in a tradition of metaphysics of the sort rejected by the empirically French *philosophes*. Kant's views matured into the colossal *Critique of Pure Reason* (1781) which systematized the limits of metaphysics and provided a critical foundation for the kind of knowledge that we derive from natural science.

I ALSO SOUGHT TO PROVIDE A FOUNDATION FOR THE REVOLUTION IN MORALITY AND ETHICS WHICH I ASSOCIATED WITH THE NAME OF ROUSSEAU.

Kant strove to reconcile the tension which had led to the estrangement between Rousseau and the *Encyclopédistes*. But this tension remains visible in Kant's absolute separation between what is scientifically knowable – the realm of **phenomena** or appearances – and the inner or **noumenal** realm of the moral law.

Kant's commitment to reason, peace and progress, and the sheer range of his investigations, place him in a direct line with the leading *philosophes*. But what is distinctively Germanic about Kant's critical work, and quite opposed to the inspiration of the *philosophes*, is his ambition to create a complete and comprehensive philosophical system. Kant thought that, as a result of his systematic clearing away of all previous metaphysical confusions, Truth was now a goal which might well be attained "before the end of the 18th century".

The critical path alone is still open. If the reader has had the kindness and patience to walk along this path in my company, he may now judge whether . . . that which many centuries could not achieve might not be attained before the present century runs out: namely to give human reason complete satisfaction about that which has always engaged its curiosity, but so far in vain.

What is Enlightenment?

By 1784, the Age of Enlightenment was almost 100 years old. A German magazine, the *Berlinische Monatsschrift*, asked its readers to respond to the question: *Was ist Aufklärung*? (What is Enlightenment?). There were responses from several of the leading German intellectuals, among them Immanuel Kant, by now famous as a professor of philosophy.

Enlightenment is man's release from his self-inflicted immaturity. Immaturity here means man's inability to make use of his intelligence without direction from another.

"*Sapere aude!* Dare to know! Have the courage to use your own reason!" This is Kant's motto of enlightenment. Kant's words summed up a vision that was shared by many of the leading intellectuals and scholars of the 18th century. And he goes on to ask, what kind of political restrictions constitute an obstacle to enlightenment?

*The **public use of one's reason** must always be free, and it alone can bring about enlightenment among men.*

The Counter-Enlightenment

So great was the success of the Enlightenment that in the second half of the 18th century it is hard to find anyone who does not share its horizons and its prejudices. Reaction to the Enlightenment's confidence in reason came not only from orthodox religion, but from "God-intoxicated" visionaries like Hamann and Blake who have had a lasting, if subterranean, influence.

No one was more fierce in his opposition to the prevailing cult of reason than **William Blake** (1757–1827). Blake was as enthusiastic about the French Revolution as he was anguished about the Industrial Revolution. He denounced the "dark, satanic mills" and the human misery suffered by the huddled masses of industrial workers. In 1789, the year of the French Revolution, William Blake published his *Marriage of Heaven and Hell*, an intense poetic handbook of anti-rational wisdom.

In his annotations to Sir Joshua Reynolds' *Discourses*, Blake reacted vehemently against the Enlightenment treatment of the imagination. According to Blake, Reynolds based himself on Edmund Burke's treatise on the Sublime, which in turn was based on the philosophy of Bacon and Locke.

They mock Inspiration and Vision. Inspiration & Vision was then, & now is, & I hope will always Remain, my Element, My Eternal Dwelling place . . . Meer Enthusiasm is the All in All! Bacon's Philosophy has Ruin'd England and Destroy'd Art and Science.

". . . May God us keep
From single Vision and Newton's sleep!"
– William Blake in a letter to Thomas Butts, 22 November 1802

In the apocalyptic language of his visions, Blake diagnosed a society
fatally mechanized, whose materialist and determinist ideas reduced
Man to no more than a machine.

"I turn my eyes to the Schools and Universities of Europe
And there behold the Loom of Locke, whose Woof rages dire,
Wash'd by the Water-wheels of Newton: black the cloth
In heavy wreathes folds over every Nation: cruel Works
Of many Wheels I view, wheel without wheel, with cogs tyrannic
Moving by compulsion of each other . . ."

Georg Hamann (1730–88)

In 1768, in the Königsberg garden of his friend, the English merchant Mr Green, Kant said that astronomy had attained to such perfection that no new hypotheses were possible in it. Kant, whose whole mentality revealed a craving for order, could applaud the fact that science seemed so close to emptying the mystery even of the further reaches of the cosmos. **Georg Hamann**, another Königsberg acquaintance of Kant's, not only opposed the advance but felt – rather like Blake – that he wanted to destroy it altogether.

Hamann, the "Magus of the North", attacked every cherished tenet of Enlightenment creed. He felt himself to be like a David who had to stand against the Enlightenment Goliath. As such he is a true pioneer of anti-rationalism, much admired by the Danish philosopher **Søren Kierkegaard** (1813–55).

I look on the best demonstration in philosophy as the sensible girl looks on a love letter – with pleasure but suspicion.

[Hamann in a letter to Kant]

Language, the Organon* of Reason

Whereas Blake was angry at the way in which the Enlightenment had downgraded imagination, Hamann thought that it had made itself ridiculous by overlooking the role of language.

All idle talk about reason is mere wind . . . Not only the entire capacity to think rests on language, but language is also the centre of the misunderstanding of reason with itself.

MY REASON IS INVISIBLE WITHOUT LANGUAGE . . .

I am close to suspecting that the whole of our philosophy consists more of language than of reason, and the misunderstandings of countless words, the personification of arbitrary abstractions have generated an entire world of problems which it is as vain to try to solve as it was to invent them.

*organon – a method or tool of investigation

Sturm und Drang

Despite the encouragement of Frederick II of Prussia, the Enlightenment failed to make much headway in the patchwork of German-speaking principalities. When it arrived, it was ushered in by a group of "angry young men" who created a fashion for protest and emotional intensity and turbulence. Known today as *Sturm und Drang* (Storm and Stress) after a play (*Wirrwarr, oder Sturm und Drang – Confusion, or Storm and Stress*) by **Friedrich Klinger** (1752–1831), it was known at the time as the *Geniezeit* (Age of Genius). Inaugurated by Hamann's *Sokratische Denkwürdigkeiten* (1759), it flourished only briefly in the 1770s.

I am torn asunder by passions which would overwhelm anyone else . . .
every moment I should like to fling humanity and all that lives and
breathes to the chaos to devour, and to hurl myself after them.

The great novel of the *Sturm und Drang* was *Die Leiden des Jungen Werthers* (*The Sorrows of Young Werther*, 1774), by **Johann Wolfgang von Goethe** (1749–1832). The melancholy, suicidal hero, Werther, swept much of educated Europe off its feet.

I WITHDRAW WITHIN MYSELF, AND THERE I FIND A WHOLE WORLD, ALBEIT A WORLD OF FOREBODINGS AND SHADOWY FRAGMENTS, RATHER THAN OF CLEAR-CUT IMAGES.

Die Leiden des Jungen Werthers

That novel and the movement as a whole were profoundly influenced by Rousseau. The young men of the *Sturm und Drang* despised the rationalism of the Enlightenment *philosophes* and adopted Rousseau's moralism and his religion of nature.

As they grew older, the leading representatives of the *Sturm und Drang* became the giants of German Classicism. A younger generation of writers (mixing in the same circles) became the German Romantics.

Voltaire at Ferney

Voltaire's wise financial investments and his success as a writer made him a very wealthy man. He settled again in France, but near enough to the border for a handy escape. On his estate at Ferney in the vicinity of Geneva, he built an elegant château.

From 1760, Voltaire held court at Ferney. Visitors came from every nation. He became a European curiosity, a "must see" on the Grand Tour of every educated tourist. In the hope of changing society, Voltaire continued to bombard the public with little, inexpensive books of diatribes, treatises, newspaper articles and commentaries.

Never will twenty folio volumes bring about a revolution. Little ones are the ones to fear, the pocket-size, portable ones that sell for thirty sous. If the Gospels had cost 1200 sesterces, the Christian religion could never have been established.

A One-Man Amnesty International

About fifteen million of Voltaire's written words have come down to us – enough to make twenty Bibles. Voltaire was determined to be more than just a man of letters. In this respect, he differed from Montesquieu, Diderot and Rousseau, who were content to enlighten or inflame men's minds through their writings alone.

OPPRESSED INNOCENCE MOVES ME; PERSECUTION MAKES ME INDIGNANT AND FEROCIOUS.

MY GREATEST WORK IS THAT I HAVE DONE A LITTLE GOOD.

When Voltaire discovered there were still serfs on estates not far distant from his own, he wrote in support of a campaign to free them. Despite his constant campaign in favour of free speech and religious toleration, Voltaire was not really a social reformer. He took up individual "lost causes"; he defended anyone whom he believed had been the victim of injustice, prejudice or religious bigotry. An admirer wrote that Voltaire's attitude might be summarized as: "I disapprove of what you say, but I will defend unto the death your right to say it."

"What does it mean to be free?" Voltaire asked. "It means to reason correctly, to know the rights of man; and when they are well known, they are well defended."

The *Canaille*

There was one subject on which Voltaire – like all the other *philosophes* – wavered: the treatment of the masses. Diderot's writings offer a depressing anthology on the theme of the mob as a fact of life. No one fully faced, let alone resolved, the problems raised for political theory by the dangers and opportunities of **education**. "The people is too idiotic, too beastly, too miserable and too busy to enlighten itself," Diderot wrote in a letter to Sophie Volland, 30 October 1759. In the entry "*Encyclopédie*" in the *Encyclopédie* itself, a strategic place to make such a remark, Diderot wrote . . .

The general mass of the species is made neither to follow, nor to know, the march of the human spirit.

More than half the habitable world is still populated by two-footed animals who live in a horrible condition approximating the state of nature . . . living and dying practically without knowing it.

AS FOR THE *CANAILLE*, I HAVE NO CONCERN WITH IT; IT WILL ALWAYS REMAIN *CANAILLE*.

Voltaire could not have foreseen that this *canaille* – "the rabble", with its deeply resentful, educated underclass – which he dismissed in 1767 would soon provide the breed of *sans-culottes*, the extremist republicans of the French Revolution.

Crisis in the Old Régime

When the young Louis XVI came to the throne in 1774, one of his first appointments was the *philosophe*, **Anne-Robert Jacques Turgot** (1727–81), who had a distinguished career of public service. Turgot developed a programme of economic reform.

After less than two years, Turgot was dismissed. The *philosophes* were dismayed. For half a century, they had looked to argument and criticism to foster a spirit of reform. But even such a respected and experienced figure as Turgot could not survive the opposition of entrenched reactionary forces. As Voltaire said, "The dismissal of that great man, Turgot, crushes me. Since that fatal day, I have not followed events or asked anyone for anything. I am patiently waiting for someone to cut our throats."

The French Revolution

In 1789, in a desperate attempt to deal with financial crisis, Louis XVI was forced to summon the Estates-General, a national assembly representing the three divisions in French society: the clergy, nobility and common people. The Estates-General had not met for 175 years. Fierce disputes over how the assembly should conduct its business led to popular agitation and finally to revolutionary action. The commoners broke away to form their own National Assembly.

On 14 July 1789, the Parisian crowd stormed the Bastille. By the end of August, the traditional feudal privileges of the French aristocracy had been swept away and the "Declaration of the Rights of Man and of the Citizen" had become law. The natural rights of man were declared to be sacred and inalienable: ". . . liberty, property, security and resistance to oppression".

In the Declaration, the ideals of the Enlightenment were encoded and offered to the world. For the next ten years, France was racked by revolutionary violence and forced to defend itself from attacks from the rest of Europe. Napoleon's accession to power in 1799 meant that the Revolution, and with it the transformed legacy of the Enlightenment, went over to the offensive.

The End of the Enlightenment

Very few of the *philosophes* who had created the Enlightenment lived to see the French Revolution. The revolution was made by much younger men, and in its extreme form by such Jacobin leaders as **Maximilien Robespierre** (1758–94), and **Louis-Antoine Léon de Saint-Just** (1767–94), the architects of the Reign of Terror (1793–94), who saw themselves as devotees of Rousseau.

In a speech on 7 May 1794, Robespierre set out to avenge Rousseau against the sophisticated *philosophes* who were alleged to have persecuted him.

FRANCE WILL BE MORALLY REGENERATED WHEN THE REPUBLIC DEDICATES ITSELF TO A SUPREME BEING AND HAS MADE VIRTUE THE CRITERION OF EVERY ASPECT OF PUBLIC LIFE.

Robespierre

Saint-Just

Rousseau had written of Virtue as the "sublime science of the simple soul"; and his novel *Emile* opens with the words, "All is good as it leaves the hands of the Author of all things, all degenerates in the hands of men."

The Apotheosis of Jean-Jacques

Soon after his death in 1778, Rousseau, who had been shunned by so many during his life, was already acquiring the halo of immortality. A statue had been erected in Geneva. In 1781, a collection of melodies by Rousseau was published and the proceeds donated in the name of his widow to the Foundling Hospital. Among the subscribers were Queen Marie-Antoinette and Benjamin Franklin.

IN *1782*, I VISITED ROUSSEAU'S GRAVE AT ERMENONVILLE, 25 MILES OUTSIDE PARIS.

Rousseau's paranoid conviction that he was persecuted by jealous *philosophes* fed the alienation of many writers who believed themselves unappreciated by the Parisian literary establishment. Rousseau became the Divinity of this literary underclass, typified by Robespierre and other radicals. Spurned, mistreated and nomadic, Rousseau was at once their consolation and their prophet.

The Ideal Republic

A year after the fall of the Bastille, at the Festival of Triumph on 14 July 1790, the bust of Jean-Jacques crowned with laurels was paraded through the streets of Paris, attended by 600 white-gowned girls and troops of guardsmen, their firearms wreathed in flowers. In October, his ashes were brought from Ermenonville to be consecrated in the Panthéon.

Political action and public debate were fused in a process which, although completely unforeseen by the *philosophes,* was nevertheless inspired by them. But war threatened the revolution from without; petitions carrying the angry demands of the poor made it vulnerable from within. Soon every principle was subordinated to national survival. The Republic introduced a democratic franchise, imposed price controls in the interests of the urban poor, and unleased the Reign of Terror against the "enemies of the Republic".

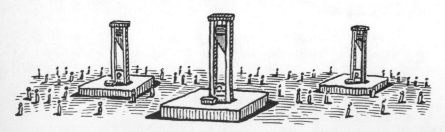

Despite the radicalism of his philosophical analyses, Rousseau was anything but a political activist. He feared the political upheavals which he foresaw. Robespierre and Saint-Just, who believed themselves faithful to Rousseau, saw revolutionary France as the reincarnation of the embattled Ideal City of Rousseau's dreams. The actual struggling republic became the locus of a new "moral" community.

Between April and June 1794, the revolutionary tribunal condemned some 1,400 people to the guillotine.

The Enlightenment Project – Finished or Unfinished?

Enlightenment principles of order and progress, confidence in the possibility of controlling nature and history, trust in commonsense and universal human nature, can be made to sound pompous, questionable or even dangerously misleading. The 19th century caricatured those principles in the wake of Romanticism and revolution. Our own postmodern age, in the famous words of Jean-François Lyotard, has witnessed the collapse of the "grand narratives" which enshrined those sweeping principles. Is the Enlightenment project over? Or is it unfinished?

The French Revolution was experienced throughout Europe as the most profound spiritual and intellectual crisis. The sense of common purpose which characterized Enlightenment intellectuals was displaced by division and conflict. The moment of rupture and renewal was spiritualized (and harmonized) in Romanticism (and in Hegel's philosophy). The 19th century adhered to the "grand narratives" by its own attempts to reconstitute a continuum of gradual progress in the new scientific paradigms of positivism, socialism and evolutionism, which were believed truly "modern".

The men of the Enlightenment defined themselves as "modern", and were the first to explore in detail what that meant. Their modernity has a naive, almost childlike innocence to it. From the Revolution of 1789 to the "bloodless" revolutions of 1989 – and through centuries of exploitation, war and colonial conquest – modernity has remained painfully entangled with bloodshed and terror. No wonder that in recent decades intellectuals have attempted to recreate a sense of innocence and playfulness by calling themselves "postmodern".

Ours is NOT an enlightened age. Fundamentalism, superstition, cynicism and fear seem to be gaining ground. But we are still all children of the Enlightenment. Our situation may be more complex and our intellectual resources more refined, but we face dilemmas which would be familiar to a Diderot, a Voltaire or a Rousseau. Only of this could Diderot and the others be sure: one had to dare to face the questions, rely on one's powers of reflection and be ready to re-think everything.

"The central issue of philosophy and critical thought since the 18th century has always been . . . What is this Reason that we use? What are its historical effects? What are its limits, and what are its dangers?"
>   Michel Foucault, in an interview,
>   "Space, Knowledge and Power" (1982)

The German social theorist Jürgen Habermas is probably the most eloquent defender of the contemporary relevance of the Enlightenment project.

"Enlightenment thinkers still had the extravagant expectation that the arts and sciences would promote not only the control of natural forces, but would also further understanding of the world and of the self, would promote moral progress, the justice of institutions, and even the happiness of human beings. The 20th century has shattered this optimism . . . Should we try to hold on to the *intentions* of the Enlightenment, feeble as they may be, or should we declare the entire project of modernity a lost cause?"

Habermas, "Modernity versus Postmodernity" in *New Left Critique*, 22 (Winter 1981)

The Polish-born sociologist Zygmunt Bauman is one of many contemporary thinkers who caution against any over-hasty identification with the hopes and aspirations of the Enlightenment. Bauman sees "modernism" as the long history of that militant stance among intellectuals which expressed their claim to be able to legislate for the whole of society, and in so doing to "solve" the problems thrown up by "modernity" (i.e. the evolution of a commercial, technological and fragmented society). Bauman sees the search for "solutions" and the arrogance of intellectual "legislators" as implicated in many of the horrors of modernity, including the Holocaust. In Bauman's account, what is positive about the shift to "postmodernism" is the recognition it embodies that we must learn to live with social change and social problems, and that intellectuals can play a more modest but more helpful role as "interpreters" of our confused and confusing world.

We can get on friendly terms with the Enlightenment. Radical postmodern reflections lead us back to the Enlightenment, in which we can recognize the very foundations of our way of understanding the world. Like ours, it was an age when certainties and long-standing stability dissolved. We need its example, just as the Enlightenment thinkers needed the example of their beloved Romans, Cicero and Seneca. As they struggled to re-think the world in secular terms, men like Diderot were fascinated by the last great pagan thinkers in the years of the "decline and fall" of the Roman Empire. As Montesquieu remarked: the ancients were "living books" – they had *known* history, whereas the moderns merely *owned* history.

Further Reading

Translations of the major works of the Enlightenment are readily available: Diderot's *Rameau's Nephew* and *This is Not a Story* (Oxford UP, Oxford & New York 1993); his *Selected Writings on Art and Literature*; Voltaire's *Letters on England* and *Candide* (Oxford UP, Oxford & New York 1990); Rousseau's *Reveries of a Solitary Walker* and *Discourses*; Montesquieu's *Persian Letters*; Hume's *Selected Essays* (Oxford UP, Oxford & New York 1993). (All Penguin UK/Viking USA except the three OUP titles listed above.)

Anthologies
There are many anthologies of Enlightenment writings. My favourite is *The Portable Enlightenment,* ed. I. Kramnick (Penguin/Viking 1995); also *The Age of Enlightenment,* ed. L. Crocker (Macmillan, London 1969); *The Age of Enlightenment,* 2 vols., ed. S. Eliot, B. Stern (Open UP, London 1979); *The Age of Enlightenment,* ed. I. Berlin (Oxford UP, Oxford & New York 1979).

General Works
Peter Gay's *The Enlightenment, an Interpretation* (1969) is a treat (reissued by W.W. Norton, New York 1996: vol. 1, *The Rise of Modern Paganism*; vol. 2, *The Science of Freedom*). Ernst Cassirer's *The Philosophy of the Enlightenment* (1932) is a highly readable classic (Princeton UP, 1969). Norman Hampson's *The Enlightenment* (Penguin, Harmondsworth 1968) gives a clear insight into changes in scientific, social and political thought. There are still many surprises in Paul Hazard's *The European Mind 1680–1715* and *European Thought in the Eighteenth Century* (both Penguin, Harmondsworth 1968). Insights on recent scholarship are offered by Dorinda Outram, *The Enlightenment* (Cambridge UP, Cambridge & New York 1995) and Roy Porter, *The Enlightenment* (Macmillan Educational, Basingstoke 1990). Dena Goodman's *The Republic of Letters* (Cornell UP, Ithaca & London 1994) gives a cultural history of the French Enlightenment.

Biographies
Diderot has two prize-winning biographies: by A.M. Wilson (Oxford UP, New York 1972) and P.N. Furbank (Secker & Warburg, London 1992). There are shorter biographies by Peter France (Oxford UP, Oxford 1983) and Otis Fellows (G.K. Hall, Boston, Mass. 1977), and a selection of Diderot's *Letters to Sophie Volland,* trans. Peter France (Oxford UP, Oxford 1972).

Gustave Lanson's *Voltaire* (1906) was reissued with an introduction by Peter Gay (John Wiley, New York & London 1966). A new short biography is H.T. Mason's *Voltaire, A Biography* (Granada, London 1981). Nancy Mitford's *Voltaire in Love* (Hamish Hamilton, London 1957) is a good way to get to know Voltaire's fascinating lover, Mme du Châtelet.

The best biography of Rousseau is by Maurice Cranston, in 3 vols.: *Jean-Jacques*; *Noble Savage*; *The Solitary Self*; (Allen Lane, London 1987, 1991, 1997 respectively). Mark Hulliung's *Autocritique of the Enlightenment: Rousseau and the Philosophes* (Harvard UP, Cambridge, Mass. & London 1994) is a brilliant study. *Rousseau* by Robert Wokler (Oxford UP, Oxford 1995) is also excellent. The essay on Rousseau in Paul Johnson's book *Intellectuals* (Weidenfeld & Nicholson, London 1988) is worth reading.

Montesquieu: a Critical Biography by R. Shackleton (Oxford UP, Oxford 1969) remains a classic. *D'Holbach's Circle: an Enlightenment in Paris* (Princeton UP 1977) shows the group that supported the most radical atheist of the age.

The Life of David Hume by E.C. Mossner (Clarendon Press, Oxford 1980) is the standard biography. *Wealth and Virtue: the Shaping of Classical Political Economy in the Scottish Enlightenment*, ed. M. Ignatieff & I. Hont (Cambridge UP, Cambridge 1983) surveys the Scottish Enlightenment. Michael Ignatieff's *The Needs of Strangers* (Chatto & Windus, London 1984) has fascinating chapters on Hume and Boswell, and on Smith and Rousseau.

Interpretations and Reinterpretations
There is much literature on the sociology of the period. Jürgen Habermas' study of the republic of letters in *The Structural Transformation of the Public Sphere* (Polity Press, Cambridge 1989) has inspired many commentaries and historical studies of intellectual life in the period. The sociology of intellectual circles is covered in Lewis Coser's *Men of Ideas* (Macmillan, London & The Free Press, New York 1970) and in the more detailed study by Robert Wuthnow, *Communities of Discourse: Ideology and Social Structure in the Reformation, the Enlightenment, and European Socialism* (Harvard UP, Cambridge, Mass. & London 1989).

Robert Darnton's books on the life of the mind and the circulation of ideas in the Ancien Régime include: *The Business of Enlightenment: a Publishing History of the Encyclopédie 1775–1800* (Belknap, Cambridge, Mass. & London 1979), *The Great Cat Massacre* (Penguin, Harmondsworth 1985), *The Literary Underground of the Old Regime* (Harvard UP, Cambridge, Mass. & London 1982), *Mesmerism and the End of the Enlightenment in France* (Harvard UP, Cambridge, Mass. & London 1968), and *The Forbidden Best-Sellers of Pre-Revolutionary France* (HarperCollins, London 1996).

A readable history of the French Revolution is Simon Schama's *Citizens: A Chronicle of the French Revolution* (Knopf, New York & Penguin, London 1989). Hannah Arendt's *On Revolution* (Penguin, Harmondsworth 1973) contains brilliant studies of the American and French revolutions from what might be termed an "Enlightenment" perspective.

The Dialectic of Enlightenment (1947) by Theodor Adorno & Max Horkheimer (Herder & Herder, New York 1972 & Allen Lane, London 1973) considers the dark side of the Enlightenment legacy. Max Horkheimer's essay "Some Remarks on Enlightenment" (1947), translated in *Theory, Culture & Society*, vol. 10 (SAGE Publications, London 1993) summarizes what Adorno and Horkheimer saw as "self-defeating" processes of Enlightenment. These themes are reconsidered in Zygmunt Bauman's *Legislators and Interpreters* (Polity Press, Cambridge & Cornell UP, Ithaca 1987) and *Modernity and Ambivalence* (Polity Press, Cambridge 1991). The contemporary legacy of the Enlightenment lies behind *The Philosophical Discourse of Modernity* by Jürgen Habermas (MIT Press, Cambridge, Mass. 1987 & Polity Press, Cambridge 1990). In his essay "What is Enlightenment?" in *The Foucault Reader* (Pantheon, New York 1984 & Penguin, Harmondsworth 1991) Michel Foucault engages with the contemporary relevance of Kant's famous essay.

Author's Acknowledgements
I would like to thank Peter Strauss, Mike Vaughan, Mike Kirkwood and Tony Morphet, who taught in the English department at the University of Natal.
I would like to dedicate this book to my friend, Larry Welborn, a true scholar.

Artist's Acknowledgements
I would like to acknowledge the following artists as the inspiration for some of the illustrations in this book: Chodowiecki, Huber, Moreau le Jeune, de La Tour, Carmontelle. I would also like to thank Basia for her help.

Lloyd Spencer is Senior Lecturer in the School of Media at Trinity and All Saints, a college of the University of Leeds. He has written *Hegel for Beginners* and is currently writing a biographical study of Walter Benjamin.

Andrzej Krauze is a cartoonist and illustrator whose work is published regularly in *The Guardian, The New Statesman* and *The Sunday Telegraph*. He is also the illustrator of *Hegel for Beginners*.

Typesetting by **Wayzgoose**
Handlettering by **Woodrow Phoenix**
Layout assistant **Ann Course**